NORTH KOREA

NORTH KOREA

TITLES IN THE MODERN NATIONS OF THE WORLD SERIES INCLUDE:

Afghanistan	Jordan
Argentina	Kenya
Australia	Lebanon
Austria	Liberia
Bolivia	Mexico
Brazil	Nigeria
Cambodia	Norway
Canada	Pakistan
China	Peru
Congo	Philippines
Cuba	Poland
Czech Republic	Russia
Egypt	Saudi Arabia
England	Scotland
Ethiopia	Somalia
Finland	South Africa
France	South Korea
Germany	Spain
Greece	Sudan
Haiti	Sweden
Hungary	Switzerland
India	Taiwan
Iran	Thailand
Iraq	Turkey
Ireland	United States
Israel	Vietnam
Italy	Yemen
Japan	

MODERN
NATIONS
—OF THE—
WORLD

NORTH KOREA

BY DEBRA A. MILLER

LUCENT
BOOKS®

THOMSON
＊
GALE

San Diego • Detroit • New York • San Francisco • Cleveland • New Haven, Conn. • Waterville, Maine • London • Munich

On cover: A modern high-rise hotel dwarfs a more traditional
building in downtown P'yongyang, North Korea.

LIBRARY OF CONGRESS CATALOGING-IN-PUBLICATION DATA

Miller, Debra A.
  North Korea / by Debra A. Miller.
    v. cm. — (Modern nations of the world)
Includes bibliographical references and index.
Contents: Land in the mountains — Korea's rich history — Communist North Korea —
Cultural and religious roots — Life and culture in contemporary North Korea — North
Korea in distress.
  ISBN 1-59018-118-2 (alk. paper)
  1. Korea (North)—History—Juvenile literature. 2. Communism—Korea (North)—History—
Juvenile literature. [1. Korea (North)] I. Title. II. Series.
  DS935.25.M55 2004
  951.93—dc22
                                       2003017111

CONTENTS

INTRODUCTION

TROUBLE IN THE LAND OF MORNING CALM

According to an ancient Korean myth, Korea is the land of morning calm, suggesting a place of peace, tranquillity, and beauty. Later, after it was subjected to repeated invasions by foreigners, ancient Korea became known as the Hermit Kingdom because of its attempts to isolate itself from almost all foreign influence. Today, although parts of North Korea remain quite beautiful and the country is almost completely isolated from the outside world, North Korea is neither peaceful nor calm. Instead it has become known as one of the most desperate, belligerent, and volatile countries in the world.

Situated in northeastern Asia, the Korea Peninsula was undivided for much of its five-thousand-year history. In 1910, however, Japan colonized Korea, beginning a four-decade period of brutal exploitation and repression for the Korean people. After Japan was defeated in World War II, the United States and the Soviet Union liberated Koreans from Japanese rule but divided the peninsula into two separate countries. In this way, North Korea became a Soviet-sponsored Communist nation formally called the Democratic People's Republic of Korea (DPRK).

The foreign-imposed division of Korea has contributed immeasurably to modern North Korea's attitudes and policies. Since its inception in 1948, for example, North Korea's major foreign policy goal has been to reunite with South Korea. In 1950, the North invaded the South in an attempt to force a military consolidation of the two countries, which began the Korean War. An international conflict between America and the Soviet Union (and later, China) was sparked when those countries became involved in the war. Although the war did not achieve its goals of reunification, North Korea built up its military and continued its plans for Korean unity. These plans took the form of a decades-long guerrilla war against South Korea, which was characterized by acts of violence and sabotage. This was part of a strategy to destabilize the South and inspire a revolution that would, it was hoped, unify Korea under Communist rule.

Meanwhile, in the half century since the Korean War ended, North Korea developed as a uniquely Korean Communist dictatorship but remained dependent upon aid and support from the Soviet Union. Combining Communist ideas and traditional Korean values into a political theory known as *Juche*, North Korea's "Great Leader," Kim Il Sung, created a country whose people are completely isolated from the world. The government controls all types of culture and virtually every aspect of everyday life, and loyalty to the regime and military power are exalted above all else. In North Korea, ancient Korean cultural influences and traditional Korean ways took second place to the worship of Kim Il Sung. Today, North Korea retains all of these qualities and is led by Kim Il Sung's son, Kim Jong Il.

After the collapse of the Soviet Union and many other Communist countries in the early 1990s, North Korea became one

Although North Korea is regarded as a belligerent Communist nation, the vast majority of its population leads a simple life of subsistence farming.

The government of North Korea allocates a large percentage of the country's resources to its military. North Korea maintains the world's fifth-largest armed force.

of the last remaining Communist nations in the world. Consequently, contemporary North Korea, primarily because it lost critical aid and benefits from the Soviet Union when that country dissolved, faces devastating economic problems that are causing mass starvation and deterioration of its society. Despite its desperate need for international help, North Korea has refused to break from its isolation or implement major economic reforms. It continues to direct its meager resources toward military goals, maintaining the fifth-largest armed force in the world. In addition, despite some limited efforts to engage South Korea, North Korea treats most other countries in a confrontational manner, making threats of violence and war, depicting foreigners as evil, and acting with hostility in negotiations and other contacts.

Indeed, in recent years, North Korea has created international crises by seeking to develop nuclear weapons and other weapons of mass destruction and by selling missiles and missile technology to rogue nations. The United States and other countries consider such actions to be threats, not only to South

Korea and Asia, but also to the peace of the world. In 1994, for example, North Korea refused to allow international inspections of its nuclear facilities after evidence was found that it was working to develop nuclear weapons in violation of treaties it had signed. Talks with the United States defused the crisis, and North Korea agreed to end its nuclear weapons program in exchange for fuel and aid in building light water reactors for electrical production. The nuclear issue, however, reemerged in October 2002, when North Korea informed the United States that it was working on a second nuclear weapons program. Afterward, in its typical provocative fashion, North Korea escalated the crisis by restarting its nuclear plants and announcing that it already has produced nuclear weapons.

North Korea, at the beginning of the twenty-first century, thus stands at a critical crossroads in its history and culture. Its economy crumbling, its people starving, many of its traditions lost, and under pressure from the international community because of its militarist stance, North Korea's government faces many difficult dilemmas. Its choices will determine whether North Korea can eventually solve its problems, reconnect with the outside world, and perhaps someday reclaim the ancient Korean heritage of tranquillity and "morning calm."

1

LAND IN THE MOUNTAINS

North Korea is a strikingly beautiful country consisting mostly of mountains and coastline. It is located on the Korea Peninsula in northeast Asia. The small country is surrounded by larger and much more powerful nations: it shares borders with China to the west and Russia to the north, and Japan lies to the east just across the Sea of Japan. Since the Korea Peninsula was divided at the end of World War II, North Korea has occupied the northern part of the peninsula, with South Korea directly to the south. This location and geography have created a distinct Korean culture, language, and political outlook that is reflected today in the culture and politics of North Korea.

MOUNTAINS, VALLEYS, AND LOWLANDS

The Korea Peninsula is a volcanic and mountainous protrusion from the northeast Asian landmass. The peninsula's west coast is met by the Yellow Sea, and its eastern shore is bordered by the Sea of Japan. The entire peninsula is only about 150 miles wide and about 600 miles long—approximately the size of the United Kingdom. North Korea occupies about 55 percent of this territory—about the size of Tennessee or Mississippi—on the northern half of the peninsula.

North Korea's most dominant geographical feature is its mountains and deep, narrow valleys. Indeed, approximately 80 percent of the country's land is made up of mountains and uplands, created by volcanic conditions many centuries ago. As noted in a Library of Congress study of North Korea, "early European visitors to Korea remarked that the country resembled 'a sea in a heavy gale' because of the many successive mountain ranges that crisscross the peninsula."[1]

The highest mountain range is the land around Mount Paektu near the Chinese border, called the Hamgyong range. Although Mount Paektu, North Korea's highest mountain, stands 9,003 feet high, most of the peaks in this range rise approximately 4,500 to 6,500 feet above sea level. Other ranges include the Nangnim, located in the northern central part of the country; the Kangnam, which runs along the Chinese border; and the T'aebaek near South Korea, which forms North Korea's main watershed. Despite its numerous volcanic mountains,

MOUNT PAEKTU, NORTH KOREA'S HIGHEST MOUNTAIN

Mount Paektu, which means White-Headed Mountain in Korean, is the highest mountain in North Korea. It is considered sacred and is claimed to be the birthplace of Kim Il Sung, North Korea's "Great Leader." The mountain also has existed since the times of ancient Korea and has always been admired and worshipped as the place of origin for all Koreans. In addition, it has come to be known as the symbol for reunification of the Korea Peninsula, the dream of both North and South Koreans ever since they were separated into two different countries at the end of World War II.

The mountain occupies a large area, more than ten thousand square miles near the Yalu River border between North Korea and China, and it extends up to northern Manchuria in China. In the center of the mountain lies a two-mile-wide lake called the Pool of Heaven, or Chonji. It was formed after a volcanic eruption believed to have occurred in 1597, when a crater was formed that filled with water. The lake is roughly 1,260 feet deep, the deepest in the world, with steep sides, and it is filled by rainfall and melted snow with pure water that China exports as mineral water for drinking. The mountain is 9,003 feet high and is uninhabitable. Because of its height and size, the mountain became a natural boundary line between China and Korea. In 1989, Mount Paektu was made a biosphere reserve, which is a nationally or internationally protected area managed primarily to preserve natural ecological processes.

A two-mile-wide lake lies in the center of Mount Paektu.

however, North Korea occupies a very stable part of the earth's crust and experiences few earthquakes.

North Korea's mountains are known for their scenic beauty. For example, Kumgang-san (which means Diamond Mountain in English), located in the T'aebaek range, is one of the most famous mountains in Asia. It has many jagged peaks of granite that sparkle in the sun, and it has been celebrated in numerous paintings, poems, and essays. It is also one of the most sacred sites in Korea, and has been used for many centuries as a spiritual retreat.

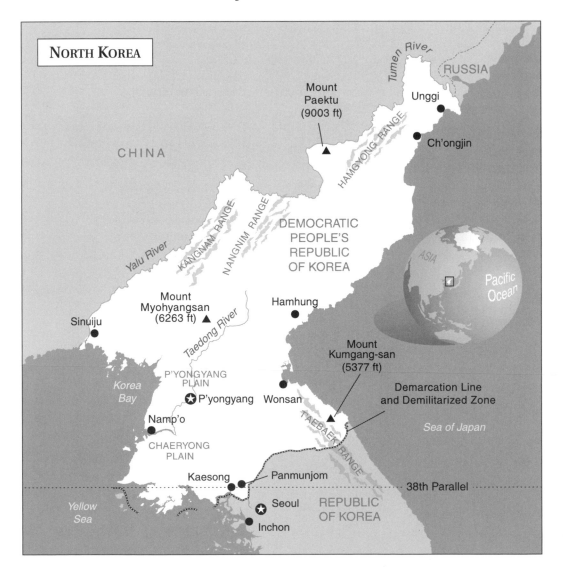

North Korea's lowlands, the only areas really suitable for habitation or cultivation, make up only a small part of the country's total acreage. Many of these plains are located in western North Korea along the coastline; in the east, the mountains drop abruptly into the sea, creating very few habitable lowlands. In addition, many of North Korea's plains, especially those in the east, are no more than narrow strips of land sandwiched between hills and high mountains. The biggest plains are the P'yongyang and Chaeryong plains, each about 193 square miles.

Although North Korea has nine separate provinces, it can be divided into three main regions: P'yong-an-do in the northwest (also called the Kwanso region), Hamgyong-do in the northeast (also called Kwanbuk), and Hwanghae-do in the south of the country. P'yongyang, North Korea's capital city, is located in the P'yong-an-do province, or the Kwanso region. This region has most of the country's flatlands and is the country's major agricultural area. The Kwanbuk area, in contrast, is very mountainous and is a center for mining and forestry. The third geographical region, Hwanghae-do province, lies to the south of P'yong-an-do province and borders South Korea.

RIVERS, LAKES, AND COASTLINE

After its mountains, North Korea's most striking characteristic is its approximately 1,547 miles of coastline. The country's western coastline is characterized by multiple indentations and irregularities, with many small islands. The eastern coastline, in contrast, is marked by steep banks and has only a few islands. Although the east coast has a few harbors, most of the useful harbors are on the western side. However, the western harbors suffer from relatively large tide fluctuations, which can sometimes vary as much as thirty-three feet between high and low tides. Low tides have often left ships and boats stranded, and in 1969 high tides caused terrible flood damage as far inland as the capital city of P'yongyang, as violent tides forced their way up the Taedong River. The major ports along the east coast include Unggi, Ch'ongjin, Songjin, and Wonsan. In the west, Namp'o and Chinnampo are the largest ports, the latter a center of trade with China.

North Korea has three major rivers: the Yalu River forms the northwestern border with China, the Tumen River forms the border in the northeast with Russia, and the Taedong River flows through P'yongyang. Nearly all of the country's rivers originate in the mountains and flow west to the Yellow Sea. Only the Tumen flows east to the Sea of Japan.

Korean rivers are mostly short, shallow, and swift, and each of the three main rivers is only partially navigable. Nevertheless, they provide waterways for commerce (particularly the Taedong) as well as water for the nation's agriculture and hydroelectric power. North Korea also is endowed with approximately 124 spas and hot springs, as well as a number of small lakes.

As has occurred in many industrialized nations, North Korea's water resources have been polluted by industrial wastes. Despite the fact that the Taedong River is the primary source of drinking water for the people of P'yongyang, both it and the Tumen River are considered to be polluted and unsafe for drinking. The pollution has helped spread waterborne diseases such as dysentery and cholera and has had a severe impact on fish populations. Similarly, marine waters in both the Sea of Japan and the Yellow Sea have been polluted by heavy metal and oil dumping by factories in cities like Wonsan and Hamhung, and from sludge that flows into the sea from mines. Many fish and marine creatures have been harmed or driven to extinction.

MINERAL AND ENERGY RESOURCES

Thanks to its mountains and rivers, North Korea enjoys abundant mineral resources and hydropower (waterpower used to make electricity). The country's mineral resources include coal, lead, tungsten, zinc, graphite, magnesite, iron ore, copper, gold, pyrites, salt, and fluorspar. These minerals have been mined and, together with hydropower, have formed the basis for North Korea's industrial development since World War II. Historically, the country's manufacturing has focused on heavy industry, especially products for military use, with light industry and consumer-goods production lagging far behind.

In addition, North Korea's coal and water resources have allowed it to produce electrical energy. Korea developed its hydropower during the Japanese occupation period, when northern Korea supplied more than 90 percent of the electricity for the Korea Peninsula. Later, in the 1970s, North Korea began focusing more on coal, which is its most abundant mineral resource. As for other energy sources, North Korea possesses no domestic oil reserves and must import oil from other countries. Another energy source, nuclear power, has

been the subject of North Korean development since the 1980s but does not as yet contribute significantly to the country's electrical power. As a result, North Korea's electricity still comes mainly from hydropower and coal.

Unfortunately, experts believe this reliance on coal and North Korea's rapid industrialization in the twentieth century have resulted in significant air and soil pollution. Because North Korean factories are not installed with filters or other tools to prevent pollution, contaminants such as sulphur and carbon monoxide are released into the air. In addition, the unrestricted disposal of industrial wastes, especially in industrial regions, has led to an accumulation of toxic pollutants in the soil and to contaminated groundwater. The lack of information from the government of North Korea makes it difficult to measure this pollution with any accuracy, but it is known that, in 1986, the government adopted environmental protection legislation designed to address some of these problems. To some extent, however, environmental pollution is limited in North Korea compared to other countries due to its partial reliance on clean hydroelectric power and due to the relatively small number of gasoline-powered automobiles and other vehicles.

North Korea's rapid, unregulated industrialization and its reliance on coal as a fuel have heavily polluted the country's air, water, and soil.

FLORA AND FAUNA

In addition to minerals, North Korea's mountains contain forests that provide a variety of trees and plant life. Trees include larch, poplar, oak, alder, pine, spruce, and fir. Indeed, as of the early 1990s, approximately 80 percent of the country was made up of forests and woodlands. Most of these forests are in the mountainous Hamgyong, Yanggang, and Chagang provinces. These forest resources were heavily damaged by overcutting during the Japanese occupation of Korea, and North Korea reforested these areas during the early years of its nationhood. These reforestation efforts, however, were dropped in the 1970s, and many forest areas have now been stripped for timber and fuel.

Similarly, North Korea's abundant coastlines, rivers, and lakes provide for fishery industries, although like timber, the fishing industry appears to be in decline. The major fishing areas are in the Sea of Japan in the east and the Yellow Sea to the west. Typical fish from eastern waters are pollack (a favorite of most Koreans), sardines, and squid. From the west, North Koreans fish for yellow covina and hairtail, and deep-sea fish such as herring, mackerel, pike, and yellowtail. Fuel shortages, pollution, and the lack of investment in equipment, boats, and facilities, however, have caused a decrease in the numbers of fish caught during the late 1980s and 1990s.

As for wildlife, large indigenous mammals, such as deer, bears, leopards, tigers, and wolves once populated North Korea, but they are becoming increasingly rare and limited to the more remote forested regions. Birds include cranes, herons, and snipes (small birds similar to sandpipers).

CLIMATE

North Korea also is blessed with a relatively temperate climate with four separate seasons, similar to that of New York City. However, the climate on the peninsula varies widely due to the influences of monsoons (storms that bring very heavy rainfall), mountains, and wind currents.

For example, the west coast, facing continental Asia, is vulnerable to the influences of cool monsoons during the year, creating more rainfall, while the east coast is protected from these northwesterly winds by steep mountain ranges. Also, because of warm currents from the east sea, the eastern part of the country tends to be a few degrees hotter than the west coast. In addition, the northern part of the country, particularly the northern mountain ranges, often experiences long and bitterly cold winters, due to freezing winds blowing from Siberia. Temperatures in these mountains, for example, can quickly drop below zero, accompanied by heavy snowstorms, while P'yongyang temperatures in January range from seven to twenty-seven degrees Fahrenheit.

Summers, in contrast, are short, hot, and humid throughout North Korea, because of moist air brought by monsoons from the Pacific Ocean. North Korean temperatures in August range between sixty-eight and eighty-four degrees Fahrenheit. Summers in North Korea also bring lots of rain; more than half the country's yearly precipitation comes from rainstorms between June and September. Spring and fall tend to produce North Korea's most enjoyable weather, with milder temperatures and less precipitation.

AGRICULTURE

Despite its plentiful rainfall, however, North Korea suffers from a shortage of land suitable for cultivation and production of food. Only 18 percent of the country's total landmass is able to be cultivated. In addition, the weather in North Korea varies,

North Korean farmers harvest rice in a paddy. Rice is North Korea's main agricultural product.

sometimes producing irregular precipitation, and the soil at higher elevations is infertile. Farming is therefore concentrated in the lowlands of the west coast, where the land is level and receives adequate rainfall and a longer growing season than the mountains. The interior of Korea and other mountainous areas cannot be used for cultivation, although they do contain forested areas for lumber. In addition, the valleys between the mountains are used for livestock grazing and fruit trees.

The main focus of North Korea's agricultural programs has been the production of rice, a staple in the Korean diet. Other important crops include potatoes, wheat, barley, millet, oats, rye, and corn. Major rice production areas are located in the provinces near P'yongyang and Hwanghae. Fruit orchards are found mostly in the Hamgyong provinces in the northeast part of the country, as well as south of the cities of P'yongyang and Hwanghae. Cattle are raised in mountainous parts of the country, and other livestock such as goats, sheep, pigs, and poultry have also been part of North Korea's agricultural output.

North Korea has made efforts to increase food production with United Nations (UN) aid and the use of chemical fertilizers and irrigation. By 1990, for example, the country had

Despite the government's attempt to encourage citizens to have large families, UN census figures indicate North Korea's population is shrinking.

more than seventeen hundred reservoirs that irrigated about 70 percent of the country's cultivated land. Unfortunately, these efforts have not succeeded in making North Korea self-sufficient. To the contrary, in recent years, the country's limited agricultural resources combined with natural disasters such as floods, droughts, and other problems, have resulted in chronic food shortages for North Koreans and a dependence on UN and other foreign food aid.

POPULATION

Like other statistics, population figures are difficult to obtain from North Korea's uncooperative government, but experts have relied on data provided by the country in 1989 to the UN in exchange for UN aid. Based on this data, demographers placed the total population of North Korea in the mid-1990s at 21.4 million. However, North Korea is believed to have excluded from its 1989 figures all males who made up its extensive military forces. As explained in the Library of Congress North Korea study, "the actual size of the 'hidden' male North Korean military had reached 1.2 million by 1986 . . . numerically the world's fifth largest military force."[2]

In addition, despite encouragement by the government for North Koreans to have large families, and policies designed to provide time off from work for mothers and day care for children, the rate of growth in North Korea's population appears to be in decline. In 1960, the annual population growth rate was 2.7 percent; in 1975, it had dropped to 1.9 percent; and in 1991, the rate remained at 1.9 percent. This decline in births has been attributed to factors such as limited housing and an expectation for women to participate equally in the labor force. Also, since 1991, the country has experienced severe food shortages and economic problems that have caused the malnutrition and death of many of its people, especially children. These problems are believed to be contributing to a further decline in population growth for North Korea.

In addition, the twentieth and twenty-first centuries have seen a large number of Koreans leaving the Korea Peninsula to take up permanent residence in other countries. During the Japanese occupation of Korea, for example, many Koreans emigrated to Manchuria, the northeastern part of China, and to the Soviet Union, Japan, and the United States. Most left for economic reasons, because they could not find work or because they lost their land. After North Korea was established as an independent country in 1948, a number of the immigrants to Japan returned to North Korea, but this trend slowed after reports came back about hardships suffered there. A further drain on the population began in the 1990s, when a small but increasing flow of North Korean refugees began crossing the border to China to escape starvation, economic problems, and political repression.

CITIES AND URBANIZATION

The people who stayed in Korea settled in the plains and lowlands and have concentrated in the country's major cities. This was largely because much of North Korea is uninhabitable, with jagged, volcanic peaks and deep snow in winters. As a result, the least populated areas are the mountainous areas near the Chinese border while the largest concentrations of people are in the area surrounding the capital city, P'yongyang, and the eastern coastal area around the city of Hamhung.

In addition, since the end of the Korean War, North Korea has experienced a pattern of rapid urbanization, in which many rural residents migrated to the cities. For example, based on statistics provided by North Korea to the UN in 1989, 59.6 percent of the population was estimated to be urban in 1987, compared with 17.7 percent in 1953. Much of this shift to urban centers appeared to occur soon after North Korea's founding as a nation, between 1953 and 1960. However, what North Korea classifies as "urban" may be different from the standard definition: apparently it includes settlements as small as twenty thousand people as urban, and even its most densely populated cities, such as P'yongyang, tend to be less densely populated than comparable areas in South Korea.

P'yongyang is North Korea's largest city, as well as its capital and economic/cultural center. It has a population of approximately 2.3 million. North Korea has made the city a showplace with a subway system, multilane highways, and many modern buildings, skyscrapers, and impressive government monuments. The country's second-largest city, Hamhung, is the capital of South Hamgyong province and is located near the east coast, north of the port of Wonsan. Hamhung (population approximately 701,000) is mostly an industrial city, but it has existed since ancient times and has a number of historical buildings. Other large cities in North Korea include Ch'ongjin (520,000), Namp'o (370,000), Sunch'on (356,000), and Sinuiju (289,000).

A VIEW OF P'YONGYANG, NORTH KOREA'S CAPITAL

P'yongyang is the capital of North Korea, and its name means "flat land" or "cozy place." It is situated along both sides of the Taedong River in the north-western part of the country, the area of North Korea known for its plains and agriculture, and it is protected by hills and mountains to the north and east. Home to about 2 million people, the city is the best-maintained and most modern place in North Korea. It has meticulously maintained parks and fountains, broad, tree-lined boulevards, and wide multilane roads.

North Korea's largest city is starkly clean and almost silent. Visitors report that there is no trash, no advertising or signs, no sirens, and virtually no traffic. Hardly any people can be seen on P'yongyang's streets, and at night, there are no lights, even in the very modern-looking high-rise apartment buildings. These seeming oddities in such an urban setting can be explained by North Korea's Communist government system and the country's declining economy. Private enterprise is disfavored in North Korea; thus, the only advertising consists of billboards and statues praising North Korea's government leaders. The lack of electricity and the absence of traffic, pedestrians, and business activity reveal the depth of the country's economic crisis, in which people cannot afford transportation or electricity and industry and work has almost stopped. One positive aspect of the capital city, however, is its cleanliness. Groups of North Korean women sweep the streets and highways constantly, and pollution is almost nonexistent.

Although P'yongyang is home to nearly 2 million people, the capital city is very clean and quiet.

TRANSPORTATION AND INFRASTRUCTURE

North Korea's infrastructure, especially its transportation system, is generally outdated and in need of modernizing. Very few North Koreans own automobiles, and railroads tend to be the main form of transportation for both commercial freight and passengers. In the 1990s, for example, according to the Library of Congress, "railroads hauled 90 percent of all freight, with 7 percent carried on roads and 3 percent of transport hauled by water. . . . Comparative figures for passenger traffic were 62 percent, 37 percent, and 1 percent, respectively."[3] Two major railroad lines run north to south, one along the east coast and one along the west coast. Two east-west lines connect the cities of P'yongyang and Wonsan, and a third east-west line connects the northern, mountainous provinces along the Chinese border.

Waterways provide some limited transportation, particularly along the coasts. Inland rivers, however, are only partially navigable and can accommodate only smaller boats. North Korea's major seaports are Namp'o on the west coast and Najin, Ch'ongjin, Wonsan, and Hamhung on the east coast. Coastal navigation is heavier on the east coast, where waters are deeper and can handle larger ships.

As for air travel, although airports exist, North Korea has very few international air connections and few regularly scheduled flights. There is an international airport at Sunan, north of P'yongyang, with flights to locations such as Moscow, Beijing, Tokyo, and locations in the Middle East and Africa. Domestic air travel is limited to a few routes as well, such as routes connecting P'yongyang with Hamhung, Wonsan, and Ch'ongjin.

Because of a lack of fuel and the almost nonexistence of privately owned automobiles, the roads in North Korea are not very well maintained. As of 1990, only a few were paved, and most are dirt or gravel roads. Multilane highways have been built linking P'yongyang with cities such as Wonsan, Namp'o, and Kaesong. Most vehicles, however, are owned and used by the North Korean military, although the country at one point had a bus service linking rural villages.

North Korea is blessed in many ways—with beautiful mountains, mineral resources, and abundant water. Yet it lacks the agricultural resources needed to produce enough food to feed its people, and without imports and economic relations with other countries, has yet to prosper as a modern nation.

Korea's
Rich History

Korea's history stretches back thousands of years and is dominated by repeated invasions from neighboring foreign powers, as outsiders such as the Chinese sought to control the Korea Peninsula. These invasions contributed significantly to Korean culture and civilization. At the same time, the repeated attacks fostered a desire for freedom from foreign rule among the Korean peoples that led to the formation of a united and independent Korean kingdom that lasted for many centuries. Events in the twentieth century, however, ended this long period of Korean self-rule, but an intense Korean desire for independence and unity continues to the present day.

Ancient Korea

Archaeologists believe that Korea has been inhabited since early Paleolithic times, more than three hundred thousand years ago. These early peoples lived in caves and survived by hunting and fishing. During the subsequent Neolithic period, tribes began to form on the Korea Peninsula, producing Korea's Bronze Age and the beginnings of rice cultivation, Korea's first agriculture. The earliest recorded Korean civilization, the kingdom of ancient Choson, appears to have been formed centuries before the birth of Christ.

Ever since these early times, Korea has been subject to invasion and subjugation by its more powerful neighbors. Indeed, Korea has been invaded more than nine hundred times in its two thousand years of recorded history. For example, the Chinese Han dynasty invaded and conquered the ancient kingdom of Choson as early as 108 B.C., establishing four Chinese-controlled colonies in the northern half of the peninsula. The Chinese could not maintain their hold in the face of Korean resistance, however, and by A.D. 313 the last Chinese colony in Korea had been destroyed.

In the process of fighting the Chinese, the Korean tribes slowly united into three separate and powerful Korean kingdoms called Silla, Paekche, and Koguryo. Koguryo initially emerged as the largest and most powerful of the three. Sprawled over a large area of northeastern Korea and extending into China, Koguryo established its capital in P'yongyang. The kingdom of Paekche developed in southern Korea near Seoul (today the capital of South Korea) and established a prosperous civilization that greatly influenced Japan. Silla was the last to develop, in central Korea, but it eventually eclipsed the other two kingdoms in power. Over a period of many centuries, each established sophisticated cultures and political structures modeled on Chinese culture. At the same time, however, conflicts

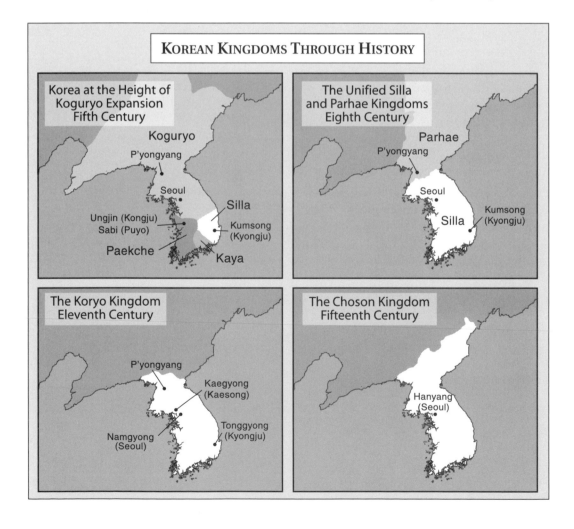

KOREAN KINGDOMS THROUGH HISTORY

Korea at the Height of
Koguryo Expansion
Fifth Century

Koguryo

P'yongyang

Seoul

Silla

Ungjin (Kongju)
Sabi (Puyo)

Kumsong
(Kyongju)

Paekche

Kaya

The Unified Silla
and Parhae Kingdoms
Eighth Century

Parhae

P'yongyang

Seoul

Kumsong
(Kyongju)

Silla

The Koryo Kingdom
Eleventh Century

P'yongyang

Kaegyong
(Kaesong)

Namgyong
(Seoul)

Tonggyong
(Kyongju)

The Choson Kingdom
Fifteenth Century

Hanyang
(Seoul)

THE MYTH OF KOREA'S BIRTH

The oldest myth about the origins of Korea is the story of Tangun, who founded the ancient Korean kingdom of Choson almost five thousand years ago. The myth was first recorded in writing by a priest in A.D. 1289. This myth of ancient Choson is revered by all Koreans as the event that first tied Koreans together by blood and culture and established Korea as the oldest continuous civilization in the world.

According to the legend, God permitted his son, Hwan-ung, to come to Earth in order to create a nation. King Hwan-ung was a good ruler. In his kingdom, there were a bear and a tiger who wanted to become human. The king told them that he would grant this wish if they stayed in a cave for one hundred days. The bear survived this test and became a beautiful woman, but the tiger failed. The bear-woman married King Hwan-ung and bore a son called Tangun. When Tangun grew up, he traveled south and built his own city at the site of present-day P'yongyang (now North Korea's capital). Tangun named his kingdom Choson, which means land of "morning calm."

emerged among the three kingdoms as each sought to expand its territory and influence.

In the late sixth century, all three kingdoms were once again faced with Chinese aggression. However, Silla, with help from the Chinese, eventually defeated both Paekche and Koguryo and then ousted the Chinese invasion forces. By the end of the seventh century, Silla formed the first united Korean government and created a prosperous and advanced civilization that lasted for two and a half centuries. Koreans during this time developed a reputation for excellence in the areas of the arts, religion, commerce, and education. Silla also maintained close political ties with China, which never attacked the peninsula during this period.

At the time of Silla's victory over Koguryo in 668, however, a Koguryo general led a group of Koguryo people to Chinese territory and founded a separate Korean state called Parhae, which later took over some of the former Koguryo land from Silla. Parhae came to control the northern part of Korea, as well as territory in China, at the same time that Silla controlled Korea south of P'yongyang. Parhae fell in 926, but in its place a new kingdom emerged, called the kingdom of Koryo, from which modern Korea gets its name. After the kingdom of Silla began to decline due to internal problems, it was defeated by Koryo in 935. However, Koryo's king, Wang Kon, treated the Silla people with great generosity, uniting the new kingdom

HAN'GUL, KOREA'S WRITTEN LANGUAGE

Han'gul (called *Choson-gul* in North Korea) is the native Korean written language favored by the government of North Korea. It was developed during Korea's "golden age," which included the reign of King Sejong over the ancient Korean kingdom of Choson between 1418 and 1450. King Sejong's rule was marked by many progressive ideas in various areas such as economics, science, music, and government, but perhaps his most well-known achievement was the development of *han'gul* to provide a written script for the Korean language.

Before *han'gul* was invented, Koreans had no written language and had to rely upon Chinese characters for writing purposes, a system that was laborious and difficult to learn. King Sejong's idea was to create a system of writing Korean phonetically (based on the way the words sounded), so that all Koreans, even ordinary people, could become literate. Accordingly, the king created a committee of scholars to work on the project, and the result was a system of seventeen consonants and eleven vowels (which was later changed to fourteen consonants and ten vowels) created in 1446. *Han'gul* is considered by modern linguists to be one of the simplest and most scientific alphabets ever devised. Its invention led to the birth of Korean literature as well as the translation of many Chinese texts.

Students practice writing han'gul, *the native Korean written language favored by North Korea's government.*

and creating another long period of peace, prosperity, and cultural achievements. Unfortunately, Koryo itself began to weaken in the thirteenth century due to brutal Mongol invasions and repeated Japanese raids.

Eventually, Korea entered its golden age—a 518-year period of prosperity under the Yi, or Choson, dynasty, named after ancient Choson and founded by General Yi Song-gye in 1392. During this time, Korea experienced some of its most celebrated social and cultural achievements. During the reign of King Sejong, from 1418 to 1450, for example, the Korean system of writing known as *han'gul* was created. Other achievements included the invention of the sundial and a model of the solar system, the creation of a notation system for Korean music and many new techniques for painting and art, the development and publication of medical theories, and the publication of the world's first known encyclopedia.

Korea became known as the Hermit Kingdom during the later Choson period because it adopted a policy of isolating itself from almost all foreign influence. Unfortunately, Korea's long history of unity and independence ended when Japan annexed Korea in 1910, making it a Japanese colony.

KOREA AS A JAPANESE COLONY

Beginning in the late 1800s, various countries sought to open Korea to trade with the outside world. Korea resisted these efforts, but in 1875, Japan used its warships to force Korea to agree to Japanese trade. In response, China sought to reassert its influence in Korea, and the two countries began to compete over who would control Korea. Eventually, this competition led to a war over Korea, in which Japan defeated the Chinese. Under the terms of the 1895 Treaty of Shimonoseki that ended the war, the Chinese agreed to end their involvement in Korean affairs, setting the stage for Japanese dominance on the peninsula.

However, Russia, supported by France and Germany, opposed Japan's growing influence in Korea, and in 1904, the rivalry between Japan and Russia finally erupted into another war. Again, Japan was victorious, resulting in another treaty, the 1905 Treaty of Portsmouth, in which Russia recognized Japan's right to control the Korea Peninsula. This treaty was mediated by the United States, which recognized the Japanese takeover of Korea. In exchange, Japan promised not to interfere with U.S. affairs in the Philippines. Japan quickly took control of the peninsula, and in 1910, formally annexed Korea, making it officially subject to Japanese rule and forcing it to exist as a Japanese colony for the next four decades.

In this way, the Korean people, having fought against foreign domination and control for centuries, found themselves living under the rule of Japan. The Japanese imposed a brutal military regime that violently subjugated the Korean people and exploited Korea's resources. One of Japan's first steps, for example, was to confiscate Korean land and property through an ambitious land program. Koreans were required to prove they owned their land, but because there were no clear records of ownership for most Korean lands, much of this property was taken and awarded to Japanese companies or individuals. Many Koreans were left homeless and poor. The Japanese also forced Koreans to adopt Japanese culture and customs.

The colonial experience devastated Korea and destroyed much of Korean culture. As writer Geoff Simons explains:

> Korea was ravaged as a captive state for nearly four decades. The Korean people, repressed and brutalized, were stripped of much of their culture while their land was stolen and their buildings confiscated. Driven from their farms, the peasants either starved in a [barely surviving] economy or were coerced into mines and factories to swell private wealth or to fuel Japanese imperial ambitions. [4]

KOREAN RESISTANCE AGAINST THE JAPANESE

Koreans resisted the Japanese just as they had resisted previous invaders. The Korean movement against Japanese rule first emerged on March 1, 1919, the day scheduled for the funeral of King Kojong, the last effective Korean king from the kingdom of Choson. On that day, Koreans from all levels of society joined together in a massive, nationwide protest, which became known as the March First Movement. An independence declaration signed by prominent Korean landowners, intellectuals, religious leaders, and others was read aloud in the city of Seoul. The declaration called for peaceful public marches and appeals to foreign powers for assistance in achieving Korean independence. Thereafter, demonstrators in towns across Korea assembled to read the declaration, wave their Korean flags, and shout their support for independence. As many as half a million people actively participated in the

demonstrations and more than a million became members of the movement.

However, the Japanese quickly and ruthlessly suppressed the demonstrations. They arrested movement leaders and fired their guns into unarmed crowds, killing and wounding tens of thousands. The resistance movement never received the expected support from foreign nations, and many Korean leaders of the independence movement were forced to flee Korea and live in exile. Yet, as the Korean Overseas Information Service explains, the movement was a success because it "greatly developed the spirit of national unity . . . and revealed to the world the true nature of Japanese rule in Korea."[5]

Thereafter, some leaders from the March First Movement established a government in exile based in Shanghai, called the Provisional Government. Under the leadership of prominent nationalists such as Dr. Syngman Rhee, the Provisional Government tried to persuade sympathetic foreign governments to come to the aid of the Korean people. These nationalists, however, remained in exile, separated from Koreans at home, and the Provisional Government ultimately failed to achieve its goal of attracting assistance from the United States and other powerful countries.

This nineteenth-century painting depicts Japanese soldiers breaking through P'yongyang's city gates. Japan took control of the Korea Peninsula in the late 1800s.

Another branch of Korean leaders remained in Korea and continued to protest Japanese rule. This was a faction that included many organizations of workers, peasants, students, and intellectuals within Korea who were drawn to the ideas of communism, a system of government that was then being promoted by revolutionaries in Russia. Essentially, under communism, an authoritarian government owns all property and controls the economy and all means of production, in theory distributing food and goods equitably to those who need them, regardless of wealth. Unlike the more distant Provisional Government, these Communist groups remained active in Korea, organizing numerous peasant uprisings, student protests, worker strikes, radical reading groups, and political protests. One branch of Communists in 1925 founded a Korean Communist Party in Seoul, headed by Pak Hon-yong.

The Communist resistance also included exiles living in the Soviet Union and China who confronted the Japanese militarily. After Japan invaded and annexed Manchuria in 1931, for example, a strong guerrilla resistance emerged there that numbered more than two hundred thousand fighters. This group set up the Korean Revolutionary Army (KRA), which organized paramilitary units to launch strikes on Japanese military police. The KRA also established grassroots groups to help the local people and win their political support. As a result of these activities, these Communist guerrillas soon were viewed as heroes by oppressed Koreans and as a threat by the Japanese. One of the leaders of the guerrilla fighters in Manchuria at this time was future North Korean leader Kim Il Sung. He was such a threat to the Japanese that they eventually exiled him in 1940 to the Soviet Union.

This resistance to the Japanese became a central theme of Korean culture, particularly for northern Korea. As stated by the Library of Congress, "Resistance to Japan became the main legitimating doctrine of North Korea: North Koreans trace the origin of their army, leadership, and ideology back to this resistance."[6]

KOREA IS DIVIDED

The Japanese were finally thrown out of Korea by the Allied powers (the nations united against Germany, including the United States, Britain, France, and Russia) at the end of World War II in September 1945. Koreans celebrated Japan's defeat, believing that Korea would once again be independent. These hopes were based, in part, on the Cairo Declaration, an agreement signed by the Soviet Union and the United States in 1943 that proclaimed Korea should become "free and independent" after the war. However, hopes for independence were dashed in 1945 when the Americans and the Soviets instead imposed an international trusteeship plan on Korea. Under this plan, a temporary Korean government was to be created and elections were to be held within five years. In the meantime, the country was divided in half along a line called the 38th parallel and was subjected to a military occupation. The Soviet Union occupied the area above the line, while the United States occupied the zone south of the line.

Soviet troops entered the northern part of Korea shortly before Japan's formal surrender at the end of World War II. Instead of paving the way for independent elections as required under the trusteeship plan, however, the Soviets immediately began a communization of northern Korea, to ensure that this neighboring area would have the same form of government as the Soviet Union. This was the beginning of a period of history lasting almost to the end of the twentieth century, called the Cold War, in which the Soviet Union tried to spread its Communist beliefs to other countries, and the United States sought to prevent this by promoting democratic and capitalist values. To accomplish their takeover of northern Korea, the Soviets installed a leader who was popular among Koreans and at the same time agreeable to Soviet control. Their choice was Kim Il Sung, a Korean hero of the anti-Japanese guerrilla war who had been exiled to the Soviet Union. He was presented to northern Koreans as their future leader in October 1945.

The Soviets and Kim Il Sung began creating a Communist state by consolidating local Communists and local Korean people's committees into a central Communist Party. Their efforts met with very little opposition, not only because the Soviets were viewed as liberators by Koreans long oppressed by the Japanese, but also because the Soviets combined their increasing control with reforms beneficial to Koreans, including, for example, a program that distributed land formerly owned by the Japanese and Korean landlords to Korean peasants.

The United States, concerned about the Soviet policies in northern Korea and worried about the spread of communism, soon moved into southern Korea. U.S. officials imposed

direct military rule and emphasized law and order, seeking
to control the area until elections could be held for an independent Korean government. In addition, the United
States suppressed the pro-Communist forces in the south
that were clamoring for Korean independence and unity,
fearing that their efforts might lead to a Communist government in all of Korea. To counter these forces, the United
States backed the nationalists who were part of the so-
called Provisional Government and brought Syngman
Rhee, an anti-Communist, into Korea.

With the Soviets organizing a Communist government in the
north, and the United States supporting the anti-Communists
in the south, Korea quickly became divided along political
lines. As a result of these political differences, talks between the
Soviet Union and the United States failed to set up elections or
implement the terms of the trusteeship. Eventually, the United
States abandoned its efforts to negotiate with the Soviets and,
in August 1947, referred the Korean situation to the UN. The
UN set up a commission to arrange for and supervise free elections on the entire peninsula. However, the UN-sponsored
elections could be held only in southern Korea because the Soviets, believing that the UN was heavily influenced by the
United States, refused to allow the UN commission into northern Korea to supervise elections there.

The result was the creation of an independent Republic of
Korea (ROK) in the south on August 15, 1948, with Syngman
Rhee as the duly elected president. That same year, the Com-
munists in northern Korea created the Democratic People's
Republic of Korea (DPRK), a Communist government headed
by Kim Il Sung. Each government claimed to be the legitimate
Korean government and sought to reunify the Korea Peninsula
under its own political creed.

THE KOREAN WAR

After U.S. and Soviet forces retreated from Korea in late 1948
and 1949, tensions persisted between North and South Korea,
resulting in a series of border clashes between the two countries. In the face of these continuing hostilities, both sides built
up their military forces. Soviet-supported North Korea, however, grew much stronger militarily than the much weaker and
less-prepared South. A group of North Koreans worked to interest the South in a peaceful reunification, but this effort eventually failed. Finally, on June 25, 1950, North Korea's leader, Kim

Il Sung, decided to invade the South with Soviet help in an effort to reunify the Korea Peninsula.

Kim Il Sung's attack on South Korea, however, was not viewed by the rest of the world as a Korean civil war but instead as aggression by one country against another. The United States, concerned about the spread of communism in Asia, quickly came to South Korea's aid together with other UN forces, thus turning the war in Korea into an international conflict.

Indeed, only about a week after North Korea's strike, on July 7, 1950, the UN authorized a force to fight the North Koreans, with American general Douglas MacArthur as its leader. By this time, North Korean troops had already captured Seoul and were moving southward. The momentum of the war changed quickly, however, after MacArthur staged a dramatic landing behind North Korean lines at the port of Inchon in early September 1950. UN forces retook Seoul shortly thereafter, and in the weeks that followed, the U.S. and UN ground forces pushed the North Korean army back into North Korea, eventually capturing the North Korean city of P'yongyang, and even moving toward the Chinese border.

U.S. ships unload troops and equipment on the beach at Inchon in September 1950.

THE DEMILITARIZED ZONE

The DMZ was established by the armistice agreement that ended the Korean War in 1953. The DMZ is a stretch of land along the border between North Korea and South Korea that separates their respective military forces. The DMZ is 158 miles long and 2.48 miles wide. It is marked by high, barbed-wire fences and is guarded by more than a thousand guard posts, watchtowers, and reinforced bunkers. The DMZ also is highly militarized, with approximately 1.1 million North Korean troops on the northern side facing about 660,000 South Koreans and about 37,000 American soldiers in the south.

Despite the tense standoff of troops, however, the DMZ has remained relatively peaceful since its creation, with no major military encounters between the two sides. In fact, the area today has become a wildlife sanctuary. As author Don Oberdorfer describes this area in his book, *The Two Koreas,* "Ornithologists have recorded 150 species of cranes, buntings, shrikes, swans, geese, kittiwakes, goosanders, eagles, and other birds passing through or living in the [DMZ]each year, joining other year-round residents such as pheasant, wild pigs, black bears, and small Korean deer."

South Korean soldiers (foreground) and North Korean soldiers (background) stand guard near the DMZ.

On the defensive, North Korea asked the Soviet Union to send troops, but the Soviets refused, not wanting to get into a war with the United States. Instead, China, another Communist nation, came to North Korea's rescue. In fact, the Chinese virtually took over the war on behalf of North Korea, and Chinese troops forced the UN army back southward, nearly conquering the entire Korea Peninsula. UN forces, in turn, recovered, and the war dragged on until an armistice was signed in 1953, leaving the peninsula once again divided along the 38th parallel, close to the prewar division line.

The Korean War is often remembered as the first battle in the Cold War standoff between the Communist Soviet Union and the democratic United States. For Korea, the war brought only terrible destruction for the people, their property, and their land. As much as one-tenth of the entire Korean population was killed, wounded, or missing in the war, and property losses for North Korea came close to $2 billion, a lot of money in 1953. North and South Korea also remained technically at war because although an armistice, or truce, was signed to end hostilities, no formal peace treaty was ever agreed upon. As a result, both sides placed large numbers of troops near the border between North and South—an area that is now known as the Demilitarized Zone, or DMZ—and sporadic hostilities have continued ever since.

The most far-reaching result of the war, however, was that it reinforced the division between the two Koreas. As historian Bruce Cumings describes, "One of the most important consequences of the war was the hardening of ideological and political lines between North and South. . . . The thirteen-hundred-year-old unity of the Korean people was shattered."[7]

3

COMMUNIST NORTH KOREA

After the Korean War, North Korea developed as a Communist nation, its leadership and economy modeled after the Soviet Union. It became dependent upon economic and military subsidies from Communist countries. North Korean leader Kim Il Sung, however, also tried to stay independent from these Communist nations, by emphasizing a uniquely Korean philosophy known as *Juche,* which means self-reliance or independence. This combination of Communist influences and *Juche* ideals produced modern North Korea—a Communist country that is characterized by isolation from the rest of the world, political repression of the people, a strong military, and confrontational relationships with other countries.

KIM IL SUNG CONSOLIDATES HIS POWER

Both during and after the war, Kim Il Sung's first priority was to increase his political power. Although he had been selected by the Soviets and appointed chairman of the Korean Workers' Party (KWP), North Korea's main political party, his power was limited at the beginning of his rule. During this time, for example, the Soviets still exercised great influence in the country. Also, the KWP consisted of several groups or factions that competed with each other for power. These factions included the Soviet Koreans, Korean Communists from South Korea who came north to become part of the new Communist government, Korean Communists who returned from exile in China, and finally, Kim Il Sung's group—a band of Korean ex-guerrilla fighters from Manchuria who had fought the Japanese during Japan's occupation of Korea.

Kim Il Sung, however, gradually removed all persons from the KWP who might challenge his power. He did this by criticizing the Soviets and other groups and claiming his guerrilla group was the only legitimate Korean leadership. Also, he accused members of other factions of political crimes, such as failing to share his ideas, and then forced their confessions or conducted show trials, eventually expelling, imprisoning, or executing them. Indeed, by the time the armistice was signed ending the war in 1953, Kim Il Sung had successfully removed three of his major rivals.

THE RISE OF KIM IL SUNG

Kim Il Sung was born on April 15, 1912, to a poor Christian family in a rural village near P'yongyang. In 1920, the family moved to Manchuria, China, where Kim Il Sung attended a Chinese school and learned to speak fluent Chinese.

In his youth, Kim Il Sung became a hero of the anti-Japanese resistance movement. While still a teenager, he joined a youth group organized by the Chinese Communist Party. Later, in the 1930s, he became a commander of an anti-Japanese guerrilla army organized by Korean exiles in Manchuria and led a division of a few hundred soldiers. Kim Il Sung's military successes as a guerrilla fighter became well known, and he was targeted by the Japanese and eventually forced, in 1940, to flee into exile in the Soviet Union. While in the Soviet Union, Kim Il Sung joined the Soviet Red Army and started a family with his wife, who was also a former guerrilla fighter. The couple had three children, including Kim Jong Il, North Korea's current leader.

At the end of World War II, in 1945, the Soviet Union sent Kim Il Sung to North Korea to head the emerging Communist regime there. Shortly there-after, he was appointed as chairman of the Communist Party of Korea and, in 1946, placed as head of North Korea's provisional Communist government. After North Korea was created as an independent nation in 1948, Kim Il Sung was named president of North Korea and remained the country's leader for almost half a century, until his death in 1994 at age eighty-two.

Kim Il Sung ruled North Korea from 1948 until his death in 1994.

By the early 1960s, Kim Il Sung had established his complete control as dictator of North Korea. He had managed to get rid of almost all other groups, and his group of Korean Communist guerrillas from Manchuria became the majority within the KWP. Soon thereafter, Kim Il Sung began referring to himself as *suryong,* or "Great Leader," of North Korea.

KIM IL SUNG'S CULT OF PERSONALITY

As part of his program to build up his power as North Korea's Great Leader, Kim Il Sung took actions to create a "cult of personality" around himself similar to that created in the Soviet Union by its leader, Joseph Stalin. This cult of personality can

This gigantic statue of Kim Il Sung in P'yongyang is a testament to the late leader's megalomania. Kim Il Sung expected his people to worship him as a god.

best be described as an organized effort to persuade North Koreans to worship Kim Il Sung and to accept his policies without question.

Kim Il Sung began this effort with a propaganda campaign that promoted both his leadership and his personal qualities and abilities. This state propaganda program praised Kim Il Sung ceaselessly for almost fifty years, giving him almost every honorary name and description imaginable. For example, North Koreans were told he was a revolutionary hero, a patriot, leader of the Communist movement, an intellectual genius, an always-victorious military commander, a respectful son, a kind father, and the sun of the nation. His every word and comment were noted and implemented as policy without question. Great monuments were built in his honor. As of the late 1960s, for example, an estimated thirty-four thousand monuments had been built to Kim Il Sung in North Korea; many more have been built since then.

North Koreans' worship of Kim Il Sung often appeared, at least to outsiders, close to fanaticism. Indeed, many have compared his rule in North Korea to a religious cult. As analyst Don Oberdorfer describes, "the most extraordinary thing about the Kim Il Sung era was the unrestrained adulation, bordering on idolatry, built up around the Great Leader."[8]

ECONOMIC RECONSTRUCTION AFTER THE WAR

Another priority for Kim Il Sung was to rebuild North Korea and help the country recover from the Korean War's economic devastation. The war destroyed the country's industry and agriculture, as well as almost all cities, towns, and villages—in fact, by the end of the war many North Koreans were living in caves. The North, however, was able to make a quick economic recovery.

In 1953, Kim Il Sung began appealing for economic aid to two leading Communist countries, the Soviet Union and China, both of which were inclined to help other Communist states. He received loans from both countries, and China also generously cancelled all North Korean debts, including materials provided to North Korea during the Korean War. Next, Kim Il Sung reorganized the economy in North Korea as a Communist economy, over which the government has full control. Under this system, the government sets economic plans and goals and the economy does not respond to market demands as it does in a capitalist system, like in the United

States. The Soviets had already nationalized, or given the government ownership of, much of the country's industry during their occupation of North Korea, and Kim Il Sung reorganized agriculture in a similar manner, banning the private ownership of land and requiring farmers to work together in agricultural collectives under common ownership.

In addition, Kim Il Sung's basic economic policy was to give priority to the development of heavy industry, including military equipment and weaponry, which he believed would be able to produce most of the raw materials, fuel, power, machines, and equipment the country needed. Agriculture was to be the next in line for economic development, with light industry, or consumer goods, as a last priority. Kim Il Sung also later launched politically based economic campaigns for both industry and agriculture. In these programs, the government tried to increase production by urging workers to work faster and more efficiently.

In 1956, Kim Il Sung announced a three-year plan of economic development. North Korea completed the plan ahead of schedule and impressed the world with its quick economic recovery. This provided Communist North Korea with much-sought-after legitimacy as compared to its enemy, the government in South Korea, which struggled economically after the war.

JUCHE AND ECONOMIC DEPENDENCE

Along with securing his power in North Korea and getting economic recovery underway, Kim Il Sung began building a North Korean national identity. In 1955, he made his first speech about a policy of national self-reliance and independence that he called *Juche*. Some have described *Juche* as a type of extreme Korean nationalism, or national pride, that sees Korea as the center of the world.

Later, Kim Il Sung developed the *Juche* idea to mean political independence from other Communist countries. Policies were enacted to create self-sufficiency in the areas of the economy, foreign policy, and military defense. As a result of these *Juche* policies, North Korea in the early 1960s distanced itself from the Soviet Union and became closer with China, while still avoiding aligning itself politically or in foreign policy with either of these two countries.

The Juche Tower in P'yongyang was built to symbolize Kim Il Sung's policy of national self-reliance and complete independence.

In reality, however, *Juche* did not fully succeed in making North Korea independent. While promoting *Juche* ideas of independence and self-sufficiency, Kim Il Sung remained dependent on economic aid and protection from the Soviet Union and China, largely by exploiting the differences between the two countries and playing one against the other. For example, in addition to acquiring aid from both countries to finance reconstruction, North Korea in 1961 convinced both the Soviets and China to sign mutual defense treaties promising to come to North Korea's aid in case of military attack by South Korea. North Korea's ability to garner support from both countries was possible largely because of competitive tensions between China and the Soviet Union created during 1956–1957, when China pulled away from the Soviet Union's domination and asserted itself as a separate Communist power center.

Ultimately, while North Korea often leaned toward China politically, the Soviet Union became North Korea's primary economic supporter. Except for a period in the early 1960s when the Soviets cut off aid to North Korea, the Soviet Union was a constant source of support. Indeed, it has been estimated that almost 50 percent of the foreign assistance given to North Korea between 1946 and 1984 came from the Soviet Union, with only about 18 percent from China, and the rest from various Eastern European Communist countries.

NORTH KOREA'S MILITARY BUILDUP

Kim Il Sung's postwar plan for North Korea also emphasized a buildup of the country's military and an aggressive foreign policy. Given the continuing tensions with South Korea following the Korean War, it seemed possible that war could erupt again between the two sides. Kim Il Sung wanted to be ready to win any such war.

Kim Il Sung's plan for the military identified four military goals. The first of these goals was to arm the entire population, as part of a national defense system in which not only soldiers but everyone could fight to defend the country. A second goal was to fortify the entire country by preparing underground shelters, weapons facilities, and factories, and dispersing them around the country. Third, Kim Il Sung ordered that every soldier be trained to perform not only his own duties but the duties of his superior, so that the army could be expanded quickly in case of an emergency. Finally, North Korea adopted a policy of constantly modernizing its military weapons and equipment, in order to maintain the most advanced military possible.

To accomplish these goals, North Korea invested large amounts of money and enlisted and trained more soldiers.

NORTH KOREA'S MILLION-MAN ARMY

Since its creation in 1948, North Korea has dedicated itself to building up its military. Today, North Korea is estimated to have approximately 1.2 million troops in its army and is one of the world's most militarized nations. Indeed, U.S. officials estimate that North Korea's armed force is the fourth or fifth largest in the world and that North Korea spends more than 30 percent of its gross domestic product on the military.

According to some of the latest estimates, for example, North Korea has 4,000 tanks and 12,000 heavy guns or rocket launchers. North Korea also has developed the world's largest commando force of 100,000 special forces whose mission is to infiltrate South Korea in wartime. In addition, North Korea's missiles are aimed at air bases in South Korea and Japan, and much of its artillery is positioned near the DMZ, where it can strike not only South Korean and U.S. troops but also the 10.6 million people who live in Seoul, South Korea's capital city.

Many downplay North Korea's threat by arguing that North Korea's conventional military equipment is obsolete. However, others point out that its forces are tough and aggressive, with many fortified bunkers and tunnels, including huge tunnels under the DMZ that could allow large numbers of North Korean troops to move into South Korea at a moment's notice. In addition, North Korea is known to have developed at least two, and possibly more, nuclear warheads; five thousand tons of chemical weapons; and biological weapons. North Korea also has deployed five hundred missiles, and it may already have developed a long-range missile capable of hitting the continental United States. Many of these missiles can carry nuclear, chemical, or biological warheads.

North Korea spends almost one third of its gross national product to maintain one of the world's largest armies.

Initially, North Korea received help from the Soviets, but when Soviet aid declined in 1962, North Korea implemented its own campaign to increase its military capabilities. Increasing amounts of the country's budget were spent on weapons and enlarging the armed forces, at the expense of economic development. For example, the portion of the North Korean budget committed to the military jumped from about 2.6 percent in 1961, to 10 percent in 1966, to about 30 percent in 1967. The military buildup escalated further in the 1970s, and by 1977, the United States estimated that North Korea had a larger military force than South Korea, even though South Korea's population was twice as large.

NORTH KOREA'S GUERRILLA WAR AGAINST SOUTH KOREA

South Korean students demonstrate against North Korea's seizure of the USS Pueblo *in 1968. Throughout the 1960s and 1970s, North Korea launched several attacks on U.S. and South Korean military targets.*

North Korea's primary military goal, according to Kim Il Sung, was unification of Korea under a Communist government. Although he failed to reunite Korea by force, Kim Il Sung nevertheless continued to provoke hostilities with South Korea after the Korean War. Soon after the war ended, for example, North Korea used armistice violations, border incidents, and psychological-warfare operations aimed at the South Korean troops to raise tensions and destabilize the government of South Korea. North Korea also sent military agents to infiltrate South Korea and collect intelligence.

In 1964, Kim Il Sung announced that North Korea aimed to incite a revolution in South Korea that would overthrow South Korea's government and reunify Korea under Communist leadership. Kim Il Sung wrote, for example, that the objective was "to carry out a people's . . . revolution against U.S. imperialism and fascist rule in South Korea, overthrowing the corrupt colonial and semi-feudal social system and setting up a [Communist] regime on its grave." [9] Thereafter, North Korea shifted to a more violent strategy aimed at destabilizing the South Korean government and weakening U.S. support there.

This strategy was based on guerrilla warfare similar to that Kim Il Sung had used against the Japanese, and it was carried out by numerous unprovoked military attacks against South Korean and U.S. targets. During the 1960s and 1970s, for example, North Korea launched hundreds of armed commando raids on U.S. and South Korean military targets. Just a few examples of these attacks include the sinking of a South Korean navy patrol boat, the seizure of the U.S. ship USS *Pueblo,* and in 1974, an attempted assassination of Park Chung Hee, South Korea's president, which instead killed his wife. Also, in an infamous 1976 incident, North Korean guards attacked a group of UN security workers who were pruning a tree at a UN checkpoint in the DMZ, using the workers' axes to kill two Americans and wound several others.

At the same time, North Korean agents infiltrated South Korea and tried to set up underground organizations to create support for revolution. One such organization was called the Revolutionary Party for Reunification, which recruited members, published a journal, and tried to organize support for an armed uprising in South Korea. In 1969, however, South Korea arrested, tried, and executed the group's leader, Kim Chong-t'ae, and the entire organization was destroyed.

Beginning in the early 1970s, North Korea pursued yet another strategy—negotiations with South Korea. In negotiations conducted in 1972, 1981, and 1985, however, Kim Il Sung showed little respect for South Korea and, using confrontational tactics, tried to force South Korea to agree to unification under North Korea's terms, which always meant Communist rule. One of North Korea's goals in negotiations, for example, was the withdrawal of U.S. troops from South Korea, a proposal aimed at weakening the South's military defenses. In addition, North Korean negotiators tried to win South Korean opposition political parties over to the Communist side. When the South resisted the North's proposals, North Korea resumed its military raids on South Korean targets.

As North Korea's strategy of inciting revolution began to fail, North Korea appeared to shift its strategy to place greater emphasis on assassination of leaders and strikes against other civilian targets. For example, in 1983, the North attacked the South Korean president, Chun Doo Hwan, bombing a South Korean cabinet meeting in Rangoon, Burma; the bomb did not harm Chun Doo Hwan, but it killed seventeen Koreans and four Burmese. Later in the decade, in 1987, a North Korean agent bombed a South Korean Airlines flight, killing 115 passengers and earning North Korea a place on the U.S. list of countries that practice terrorism.

NORTH KOREA'S ECONOMIC DECLINE

Largely as a result of its emphasis on military goals, North Korea's economic growth began to slow during the 1960s. North Korea increased its military expenditures at the same time as aid from the Soviets declined, dramatically reducing funding for economic and social improvements.

In response, Kim Il Sung tried to encourage workers to work harder and criticized those who coveted material rewards instead of working for love of their country. He also mobilized more women into the workforce and instituted new production quotas to try to force workers to produce more. Finally, Kim made every effort to restore amicable relations with the Soviet Union, succeeding in the late 1960s in acquiring significant new assistance from the Soviets. Even this renewed aid, however, could not turn the economy around.

In the 1970s, North Korea implemented a new economic program called the Three Revolutions (technological, ideological, and cultural) to stimulate innovation. As part of this program, North Korea borrowed from other countries to buy equipment and technology to modernize its industrial production. These government efforts to improve the economy, however, were foiled by the 1973 oil crisis, caused when rising oil prices led to a worldwide recession. Following the oil crisis, North Korea could not sell its goods and resources for enough money and was unable to repay its debts. As a result, North Korea owed Japan, Sweden, and other countries billions of dollars and became one of the world's worst credit risks.

This only added to North Korea's economic problems and forced it to continue to depend on aid from the Soviet Union and China.

POLITICAL REPRESSION IN NORTH KOREA

North Korea's government was able to remain stable in the midst of the economic downturn, largely because it prohibited any type of political dissent or challenge to its policies. Like many other Communist countries, North Korea's government is a dictatorship. The government therefore controls the country's economy, media, and justice system, with no checks and balances on its activities. This allows North Korea's leaders to impose their policies, suppress all negative reporting about their actions, accuse anyone of political crimes, and punish dissenters with imprisonment or execution.

When the Communists first organized in North Korea and began to improve the economy, their policies improved North

NORTH KOREA'S HUMAN RIGHTS RECORD

The restrictions placed by North Korea's government prevent access to the country by UN human rights experts and private human rights organizations, posing a major obstacle to efforts to monitor North Korea's human rights abuses. Nevertheless, based on interviews of North Korean refugees who have fled to China and other evidence, serious human rights abuses have been documented.

For example, both the U.S. State Department and private groups such as Human Rights Watch claim that the North Korean government makes arbitrary arrests of citizens and uses torture, imprisonment, and execution to punish people who commit political crimes. Those who become political prisoners are subjected to cruel treatment. There is no independent court system, and trials are not fair. The country's political crimes are so vaguely defined that the death penalty could be used to punish even peaceful political activities. North Korea's laws, for example, impose the death penalty for a wide variety of crimes considered to be a threat to the government, including defection, attempted defection, slander of government policies, listening to foreign radio or television broadcasts, writing reactionary letters, and possessing reactionary printed materials.

North Korea also severely restricts freedom of religion, assembly, association, movement, and freedom of the press, and it discriminates against citizens on the basis of family background and prohibits citizens from leaving the country. Anyone who leaves North Korea and is returned faces imprisonment or even execution.

Koreans' standard of living from the low level it had reached during Japan's colonial rule. However, when the country's economy stalled during the 1960s and afterward, workers' quality of life declined, as they were expected to work harder with fewer rewards. It is believed that the North Korean government then began to rely more on repression to control its population.

Indeed, since the 1960s tens of thousands of people in North Korea have been imprisoned, tortured, or killed. Those who are jailed are forced to live in horrible conditions, with little or no food, until they die a slow death. Also, North Korea isolates its population from the outside world by restricting travel, prohibiting its citizens from listening to radio or watching television broadcasts from foreign countries, and limiting the number and access of visitors who come to North Korea. By the late 1980s, under Kim Il Sung's direction, North Korea had become one of the most isolated and belligerent Communist countries in the world—and continues to be so today.

NORTH KOREA'S CULTURAL AND RELIGIOUS ROOTS

Modern North Korea's cultural roots can be traced directly to its ancient influences, including the beliefs of its tribal ancestors and Chinese ideas of religion, government, and family relationships. Today, although the government policies have diluted their influence, many of these cultural roots are still visible in North Korea. Many experts believe, however, that the state's emphasis on the cult of personality surrounding Kim Il Sung and his son, Kim Jong Il, has all but destroyed religion in North Korea.

SHAMANISM IN ANCIENT AND MODERN KOREA

Animism, or a belief that the world is controlled by spirits, is probably Korea's oldest cultural and religious influence. Korea's earliest inhabitants worshipped elements of nature, such as the sun, the stars, the moon, mountains, trees, and rivers and believed that all these parts of the natural world were inhabited by spirits, or souls. They also believed in shamans, a type of priest or medicine man (or often a woman, in Korea), who they believed could communicate with the spirit world, largely through activities such as divination (telling the future), and healing. In Korea, shamanism is called *Siny'gyo,* or Way of Gods.

Early Koreans, through shamanism, sought the assistance of spirits to help them in their daily lives. Shamans, using a type of self-hypnotism or trance state, presided over rites, ceremonies, and sacrifices held to invoke this spiritual assistance, and music and dance evolved as part of these rituals. Rites included a rain ceremony, the purification rite, the prayer for national security, and ceremonies to influence the gods that governed the fall harvests. Shamanism also provided an outlet for stress and tension, particularly for women, who primarily acted as the shamans in Korea. In addition, early leaders in Korea were often shamanic rulers; indeed, Tangun, the ruler of ancient Choson, is believed to have been a shaman.

The many rituals and symbols created by shamanism became so entwined with Korean daily life that they survived through the centuries and became incorporated into other belief systems that took root in Korea. Many cultural events, as well as common symbols in traditional Korean art and cultural lore, are derived from shamanism. For example, agricultural holidays such as Thanksgiving Day and the May Festival, on which shamanic rites were performed, became days of popular recreation even after their religious significance disappeared. Also, in the early twentieth century, screens used to decorate Korean homes often contained the ten longevity symbols (turtles, deer, cranes, pine trees, bamboo, sun, clouds, rocks, water, and what was known as the

Animism, the belief that spirits control all things, is Korea's earliest religious influence. This painting depicts the spirit of a mountain.

"fungus of immortality"). Pillowcases on Korean beds were expected to show good luck symbols (unicorns, turtles, phoenixes, and dragons), and roofs often sported animal figurines called *chapsang* for repelling evil—all magical beliefs from shamanism. Many of these folk beliefs live on in modern South Korea. However, the government in North Korea has consciously tried to uproot shamanist beliefs, and the practices and cultural symbols of shamanism seem to have largely disappeared in North Korea.

THE RISE OF BUDDHISM IN THE THREE KINGDOMS

Buddhism came to Korea in the late fourth century from China, during the period of the Three Kingdoms, and became the dominant influence on Korean thought and culture for many centuries. Although there are many different sects, Buddhists essentially believe that suffering is part of life and that people can lessen their suffering through meditation and spiritual enlightenment. The kingdom of Koguryo was initially the most affected by Buddhist thought. Later, however, Buddhism spread to the kingdoms of Paekche and Silla, and eventually became the official religion of Silla.

In Silla, Buddhism spread quickly among the royal classes, and members of the royal family became ardent followers. The Silla aristocracy were drawn to Buddhism at least partly because the Buddhist doctrine of reincarnation reinforced the strict social hierarchy in the Three Kingdoms, which was called the "bone rank" system. Under this system, which determined every aspect of Korean life from housing to job opportunities, the royal houses were at the top, the aristocracy came next, the commoners were at the very bottom, and slaves were totally excluded. According to the Buddhist reincarnation theory, one's social position was based on whether a person was good or bad in previous lives; therefore, Buddhism instructed its followers to accept their social positions and not to envy the aristocracy, providing support for the ruling classes.

For all Koreans, however, Buddhism enhanced an indigenous Korean spiritual ideal of peace and harmony that is created by individuals working together toward communal goals. This ideal emphasizes accommodation instead of individualism, and it encourages meditation as the path to growth and enlightenment. In addition, Buddhism in Korea was inclusive, accepting and synthesizing all the various Buddhist sects. As a result of the appeal of Buddhism, Silla's leaders promoted its spread throughout the kingdom.

Buddhism, however, was used in Silla primarily for political purposes. Korean kings found that Buddhism could be used to control the common people because they would more readily obey a Buddhist commandment than a political decree. Also, in addition to supporting the bone rank system, Buddhism naturally reinforced the idea of a united group of subjects serving the king, since it involved a hierarchical body of believers devoted to the Buddha, the founder of Buddhism. Silla's leaders therefore tightly controlled the temples and monks, appointed Buddhist administrators at local, provincial, and national levels, and incorporated Buddhist thought into political systems. Not surprisingly, however, Buddhism eventually became associated in the minds of ordinary people with the wealth and power of the ruling classes, causing it to decline as a religious influence during the Koryo period.

BUDDHISM'S CONTRIBUTIONS TO MODERN KOREA

Nevertheless, Buddhism survived in Korean art, literature, and philosophy and has contributed great richness to modern Korean culture. Indeed, Buddhist architecture, sculpture, and painting, along with educational and social institutions, transformed Korean culture, thanks largely to the patronage of the ruling classes who accepted the Buddhist faith.

One example of the flourishing arts during the Silla period can be found in the construction of numerous Buddhist temples, which incorporate the Chinese use of strong colors (particularly red), as well as stone pagodas, called *stupas,* which display an inverted-bowl roof design characteristic of Buddhist architecture. Another well-known type of Buddhist art is the Buddha sculpture made of stone, wood, or bronze, many of which show him seated in meditation. Also important were ceramic pottery and paintings, many of the latter depicting shamanic symbols such as turtles, tigers, and dragons or a theme special to Buddhism—ox-herding scenes, which are a metaphor in Buddhism for the human being's search for his innermost self.

Many of these Buddhist art pieces have survived through the centuries and are today prized as important cultural relics and tourist attractions. Even in North Korea, ancient Buddhist

TEN SYMBOLS OF LONGEVITY

The ten symbols of longevity form a traditional Korean motif derived from shamanism. The ten symbols are taken from nature and include three animals (turtle, deer, and crane), two trees (pine and bamboo), four landscape elements (sun, clouds, rocks, and water), and a magic fungus called *pulloch'o*. These symbols are often painted onto screens, which are used in Korean homes for important occasions, such as weddings, birthdays, and even death memorials. However, the symbols also are carved and embroidered onto articles of furniture, clothing, or countless other items, such as chests, pillowcases, shoes, dishes, and glass.

Although most of the symbols are universally recognized natural items, *pulloch'o* is a special part of Korean myth. It is shown as a fungus that grows low to the ground and looks like a miniature, mushrooming cloud. In reality, it does not exist, but it is shown in decorations as growing everywhere in the woods and peeking out from behind rocks, as a symbol of immortality.

relics are protected as examples of early Korean culture and promoted to show the superiority of Koreans. For example, Buddhist temples at Kumgang-san and Myohyang-san in North Korea have been preserved and restored, and they are considered national treasures. Myohyang-san contains eighty thousand wooden blocks onto which are carved the Korean Tripitaka, or Buddhist scriptures.

Buddhism also is reported to have made a small comeback as a religion in North Korea in recent decades. As of the early 1990s, for example, a few Buddhist temples were conducting religious services, an academy for Buddhist studies was established, and a volume of Buddhist scriptures was published. This was possible because religion in North Korea was guaranteed by the country's 1948 constitution, which stated, "citizens of the Democratic People's Republic of Korea shall have the freedom of religious beliefs and of conducting religious services."[10] However, the 1972 constitution also gave citizens the right to oppose religion, and the 1992 constitution added a provision that religion cannot be used to destroy the state or its social order.

THE RISE OF CONFUCIANISM IN CHOSON

Unlike Buddhism, which was quickly adopted by Koreans and made the state religion in the Silla and Koryo kingdoms, Confucian ideas developed slowly after their introduction into Korea from China. Indeed, Confucianism made its way into Korea at the same time as Buddhism, and existed side by side with Buddhist religious concepts for centuries. Eventually, about 150 years into the Choson dynasty, Confucianism and its later form, Neo-Confucianism, overtook Buddhism and became the official creed of Koreans.

Confucianism emphasized a hierarchy of five important human relationships: king and subject, father and son, husband and wife, elder and younger brother, and friendship. In these relationships—except for friendship, which involved two equals and required mutual respect—the person viewed as the inferior was responsible for acting properly towards his or her superior. For example, subjects were supposed to be loyal to their king, sons were to be subservient to their fathers, wives were to be obedient to their husbands, and the young were to be respectful of their elders. In addition, great importance was placed on decorum, ceremony, scholarship, and cultural education.

Confucianism also provided a clear system for the conduct of government and political affairs. Under this system, government officials were no longer appointed members of the aristocratic classes, as was the practice during the preceding Koryo period; instead, Confucian government officials were chosen by merit, through civil service examinations. This created a new class of scholar-bureaucrats, called the *yangban*, who became the backbone of political power and government rule during the centuries-long Choson, or Yi, dynasty in Korea. This Confucian merit system was a radical departure from the past and has been credited with increasing public participation in government, expanding the ruling class, and in this way creating a more stable society.

THE IMPORTANCE OF FAMILY IN CONFUCIANISM

Probably the most important of all Confucian ideals was the family relationship. The family, for Korean Confucians, was considered the basic and most important unit of society. Indeed, three of the five traditional Confucian social relationships deal with family—father and son, husband and wife, and elder brother to younger brother. Children's obedience and respect for parents and elders is probably the most important aspect of these relationships. Although these relationships are based on the idea of a superior and inferior, they also were grounded in the traditional Korean concept of the individual as part of a collective group. The Confucian ideal for family life, in fact, was "four generations under one roof," [11] referring to many generations of a family living together. Accordingly, Confucianism mandated numerous family rites and ceremonies, such as the common rites for coming of age, for marriage, for funerals, and for the dead.

A special reverence was shown in Confucianism for ancestors. It required every household to create a family shrine for the worship of ancestors, and it taught that deceased family members did not disappear or become reincarnated, as Buddhists believed, but stayed within the family circle in spiritual form.

The tenets of Buddhism have influenced many aspects of Korean culture. In recent decades, Buddhism has experienced a resurgence in popularity in North Korea.

CHRISTIANITY AND OTHER RELIGIONS IN NORTH KOREA

To a limited extent, Korea has been influenced by other religions or philosophies throughout its history, although none of these compare in importance to the role of shamanism, Buddhism, and Confucianism. By the middle of the nineteenth century, for example, a new religion emerged called Tonghak (or Eastern Learning), which was a combination of Confucian, shamanic, Buddhist, and Taoist beliefs and preached reform and emancipation for underprivileged Koreans. It also was highly nationalistic, promoting Korea as an important center of world power. Tonghak's founder, Ch'oe Che'u, however, was executed by the government in 1866, and Tonghak later was eclipsed by Western influences. Pockets of Tonghak followers exist in modern South Korea but no information is available indicating their existence in North Korea.

Also in the mid-1800s, Christianity began to flow into northern Korea from China. Catholicism was at first tolerated alongside Confucian ethics, but later was persecuted. After Korea was opened to Western trade in 1875, however, Protestant Christian missionaries flocked to North Korea, offering not only spiritual guidance but also Western education—both of which were extremely attractive to Koreans, who by then were feeling repressed by Confucian rules and restrictions. These missionaries built schools, hospitals, and orphanages and helped to modernize Korea. After the Japanese colonized Korea in 1910, Christian missionaries remained in Korea and provided spiritual encouragement to the Korean independence movement.

Today, the Christian faith survives in North Korea in small numbers. Indeed, beginning in the late 1980s, the government of North Korea encouraged North Korean Christians to reach out to Christians in South Korea and the West to promote its political goals. In 1989, a North Korean Protestant minister reported at a religious conference in Washington, D.C., that North Korea had ten thousand Protestants and one thousand Catholics. In 1992, American evangelist Billy Graham visited North Korea and spoke at Kim Il Sung University.

One other religious influence was important to Korea—Taoism. It was introduced to Korea alongside Buddhism during the Three Kingdoms period, but unlike Buddhism, it failed to take root as a separate influence in Korean culture. Taoism saw the world as made up of a duality, the two forces of yin and yang, and of five agents—wood, fire, earth, metal, and water. The central idea of Taoist philosophy, however, was to live simply and passively, in line with the flow of the universe, thereby transcending human desires and achieving harmony or oneness. Today, Taoism lives on in modern Korea, in both North and South, primarily in Koreans' love of nature and beauty.

For women, however, Confucianism provided a very limited role and low status. Although women in earlier Korean kingdoms had high status, even serving as rulers during the Silla period, under Confucianism, women were viewed as less valuable than male children from the time of birth. As adults, they were relegated to being a mere servant to men and children, and a vessel for producing offspring. Women also were expected to be obedient and loyal to their husbands no matter what. Unlike men, they were not permitted to divorce, and if their husbands died, they could not remarry. Women also were not provided with education or permitted to participate in any way in political, social, or economic life. Men were considered the head of the family unit, and they made all important decisions.

CONFUCIAN VALUES IN MODERN NORTH KOREA

Although information is limited because of North Korea's policy of preventing outsiders from visiting the country or gaining access to ordinary life, it appears that Confucian values remain a vital part of the culture in modern North Korea. Many of these values, in fact, are promoted by the state, while others have been modified by the needs and demands of the government.

For example, the family continues to be viewed by the government as an important social unit. The state encourages children to respect their parents, but this relationship is secondary to citizens' loyalty to the state. Other Confucian values, such as the father/son relationship and respect for one's elders, are similarly promoted by the government but are also used to encourage similar devotion to the government and its leaders.

Some Confucian sex roles also remain. For example, sons are still valued more than daughters, and divorce is reportedly easier for husbands to obtain than for wives. North Korea, however, radically changed the role of women from the Confucian model. In 1946, the government passed the Sex Equality Law to guarantee sexual equality for women. Later, North Korea's 1972 constitution proclaimed that "women hold equal social status and rights with men." [12] This emphasis on sexual equality had a practical basis: due to a labor shortage, women in North Korea are expected to participate in the labor market equally with men. They are provided child care by the state to enable them to work, and they are provided with education similar to that provided to males. Nevertheless, women continue to do most of the domestic chores, and they often work in jobs where they are paid less than their male counterparts.

THE CONFUCIAN ROOTS OF KIM IL SUNG'S RULE

Confucianism is probably most evident in contemporary North Korea as one of the main principles underlying Kim Il Sung's cult of personality and his ideology of *Juche*. Certain basic Confucian concepts familiar to Koreans seem to be incorporated into Kim Il Sung's political philosophy and propaganda in order to encourage political loyalty to his dictatorship.

One of the five important relationships in Confucianism, for example, is the relationship between a king and his subjects. Indeed, the political system in North Korea is often com-

A painting of Kim Il Sung's birthday celebration depicts him as a model Confucian patriarch beloved by his subjects.

pared to the human body: the country's leader acts as the brain and the people are the body that must carry out the leader's decisions and commands. A similar theme of Confucianism employed by the North Korean government is that of a wise, all-knowing father/leader who takes care of his loyal family/people, with an emphasis on the responsibility of children to be respectful and obedient toward the father figure.

For example, Kim Il Sung has been portrayed in North Korean propaganda as a kindly and wise Confucian patriarch who must receive complete loyalty from his people. As the Library of Congress study of North Korea explains, "special attention is paid to the theme of Kim's benevolence with unquestioning loyalty and devotion, recalling old Confucian values of repaying debts of gratitude."[13] North Korean biographers of Kim Il Sung have described him as endowed with all the typical Confucian virtues—benevolence, love, trust, obedience, and respect. In this way, Confucianism helped generate strong internal support for the North Korean leader. Similarly, Confucianism helped North Koreans to accept Kim Il Sung's firstborn son, Kim Jong Il, as his successor. The passage of power from father to eldest son is traditional in Confucian families, and Kim Jong Il was therefore presented as the natural replacement for the patriarchal leadership of Kim Il Sung.

Confucian values also can be seen in the *Juche* ideology. A central theme of *Juche*, for example, is the Confucian idea of family collectivism, that all citizens are part of the larger whole and must work together to promote the good of the country. Throughout its rule, the regime in North Korea has urged workers to work harder, to forget about personal gain, and to sacrifice themselves for the common good, which was always defined by the government as a national economic or military goal. North Koreans' comfort with traditional Confucian concepts of collectivism paved the way for their acceptance of *Juche*.

Indeed, it is the conservative, hierarchical, and authoritarian themes in Confucianism that seem to have been promoted in North Korea. As the Library of Congress has explained, the "authoritarian strain of Confucianism has apparently survived, transformed by socialist and [*Juche*] ideology. It appears that [North Korea] has chosen to co-opt some of the traditional values rather than to eradicate them."[14]

5

LIFE AND CULTURE IN CONTEMPORARY NORTH KOREA

In contemporary North Korea, culture is largely controlled by the government and exists primarily to enforce the themes of North Korea's political ideology and to glorify North Korean leaders. Indeed, the country's foremost cultural theme, promoted heavily by the government, is often called Kim-Il-Sungism, referring to the hero worship of Kim Il Sung. Other areas of people's daily lives, such as work, education, and food, are likewise largely dictated by the government. On the other hand, North Korea's government also has promoted parts of traditional Korean culture, such as music, dance, and painting, as a means of showing the superiority of North Korean culture to occasional visitors. The full extent of this traditional Korean culture and lifestyle in North Korea, however, can only be known if and when outside observers are granted greater access to the country.

POLITICAL CONTROL OF CULTURE

The government clearly controls culture in North Korea, and uses it to brainwash the people. Most forms of cultural expression very openly express political themes such as the heroism and martyrdom of North Korea's revolutionary struggle, the happiness of the people of North Korea, the genius of North Korea's leaders, and the evil of foreigners, especially the Americans and the Japanese. Government control is exercised through its Propaganda and Agitation Department, the Culture and Arts Department of the KWP Central Committee, and the KWP's General Federation of Korean Literature and Arts Unions (a parent body for all literary and artistic organizations). In addition, because of the isolation the government imposes on its people, North Koreans have virtually no exposure to foreign cultural influences.

The culture that is permitted to exist in North Korea, therefore, is either produced or condoned by the government. The government, for example, sends art propaganda squads throughout the provinces to perform poetry readings, plays, and songs, usually as a tool to urge workers to increase their productivity during harvest seasons. Similarly, the government encourages traditional Korean folk songs and dances, as long as they are optimistic and express themes acceptable to the regime. Themes that the regime disapproves of, such as the glorification of the individual instead of group or collective achievements, are not permitted by the government.

North Korea's regime promotes all forms of artistic expression, such as this concert of traditional music, as examples of North Korean superiority.

TELEVISION, NEWSPAPERS, AND RADIO

All forms of media—newspapers, television, magazines, books, movies—are run by the state and exist primarily as means for the government to communicate its messages to the people. For example, radio and television sets in North Korea are pre-

NORTH KOREAN MOVIES

Unlike Western movies, which cover a broad range of topics, almost all North Korean movies have nationalistic themes that portray North Korea and its government in heroic terms. There is a basic formula in which Koreans are always the good guys, triumphing over evil, which is usually represented by Japanese, American, or South Korean villains. The government regime also is obsessed with war films, especially those that glorify the North Korean military.

For example, the list of movie titles made in North Korea includes *Sea of Blood, The Fate of a Self-Defense Corps Man, Flames Spreading over the Land, The County Party Chief Secretary, Five Guerrilla Brothers,* and *The Path to Awakening.* One of the most influential films, *An Chung-gun Shoots Ito Hirobumi,* tells the story of a Korean assassin who killed a Japanese general in 1909. A few Korean folk tales also have been made into films, including, for example, *The Tale of Chun Hyang,* a story of a nobleman who marries a servant girl.

North Korean film actors wait on a movie set. North Korean film characters are always portrayed as heroes who are victorious over foreign villains.

tuned to government stations that broadcast a constant stream of propaganda. No outside programming is allowed. The "news" reports consist mainly of complimentary reports about Kim Jong Il and his daily agenda. Often he is shown visiting units of the armed forces, who are portrayed as very popular and well cared for. Television broadcasts also denounce foreign countries and leaders such as the United States and its president, George W. Bush. North Korean realities, such as the country's economic problems or the shortages of food, are simply not reported.

The newspapers in North Korea include *Rodong Sinmun* (Labor Daily), run by the KWP, *Joson Inmigun* (Korean People's Army Daily), an army publication; *Minju Choson* (Democratic Korea), also a government publication; and *Rodongja Sinmum* (Workers' Newspaper), part of the government trade union federation. In addition, there is a government-run Korean Central News Agency. Television and radio stations include DPRK Radio and Television Broadcasting Committee, Kaesong TV, Korean Central TV Station (Ministry of Post and Telecommunications), and Mansudae TV Station (a cultural station).

North Koreans are strictly prohibited from listening to or watching foreign media broadcasts. Those who are caught doing so face harsh punishments, such as forced labor. Stories from defectors, however, suggest that in the late 1990s more people were willing to risk these punishments, and some are acquiring radios that will receive foreign stations.

MOVIES AND BOOKS

Like other forms of media, movies and books in North Korea are instruments of state propaganda. Indeed, movies are considered by North Korea's government as one of the most powerful ways to educate the people about ideas the government favors. Kim Jong Il, who was in charge of culture and the arts before he succeeded his father and who reportedly sees himself as a filmmaking genius, was quoted in June 1991 on his nationalist philosophy about filmmaking: "Films should be popular and national in content and form as required by the era of independence when the [Korean] people have emerged as masters of the world." [15]

Many of these films are produced at the country's state-run motion-picture studio—the Korean Feature Film Studio— located west of P'yongyang. The studio produced its first feature film, *My Homeland,* in 1949, shortly after Kim Il Sung assumed power in North Korea. During the 1990s, the studio produced about forty films annually, with six other facilities creating an additional forty features every year. North Korean films are rarely shown outside the country, except occasionally when they are entered in Communist film festivals. However, they are widely viewed within the country, either in the state-run cinemas or on the country's state-run television stations.

Literature is another venue for North Korean politics. In fact, Kim Il Sung directed numerous novels to be written under his direction, depicting the revolutionary struggle and ideology of North Korea. These include titles such as *The Flower Girl, The Sea of Blood, The Fate of a Self-Defense Corps Man,* and *The Song of Korea.* In addition, a series of historical novels called *Pulmyouui Yoksa* (Immortal History) have been published on the theme of Korea's history as well as books such as *Korea Fights* and *The Burning Island,* both about the Korean War. The most important work of traditional Korean literature is *Samguk Yusa,* written in the twelfth century by the monk Illyon. The state controls the production of literature and art, and there is no indication that any sort of underground literary movements exist in North Korea.

ARCHITECTURE

Similarly, although some traditional Korean architecture has been preserved, most of the architecture created and condoned by the government tends to emphasize grand nationalist themes. The capital city of P'yongyang, for example, was almost completely rebuilt after the Korean War and contains the most impressive examples of this modern Korean architecture. Many of these structures are government monuments and museums dedicated to the nation's leaders and political ideology. One famous monument, for example, is the *Ch'ollima,* a sixty-five-foot-tall bronze statue of Kim Il Sung, which stands prominently in front of the Museum of the Korean Revolution, a museum dedicated to Kim Il Sung's life and one of the largest structures in the world. Both were built to celebrate Kim Il Sung's sixtieth birthday in 1972. In addition, there is the gigantic Juche Tower, which rises almost 558 feet high and was erected to honor the seventieth birthday of Kim Il Sung in 1982. Yet another well-known nationalistic structure in P'yongyang is the Arch of Triumph.

North Korean architecture also includes very modern-looking, high-rise apartment buildings and hotels. Some examples include the Ryugong Hotel, believed to be the world's tallest hotel at 105 stories, and the Koryo Hotel, which is 45 stories tall. In addition, many North Koreans reside in new, high-rise apartment buildings in P'yongyang.

North Korea, however, also has protected some traditional Korean architecture and has produced some architecture that includes traditional Korean motifs, such as tile roof designs. Several Buddhist temples and other historical buildings are shown to occasional tourists, and new buildings, such as the People's Culture Palace in P'yongyang, sometimes incorporate traditional architectural elements.

MUSIC AND DANCE

The North Korean government has encouraged certain forms of traditional Korean folk music and dance as examples of the uniqueness of North Korea. As the travel website Lonely Planet describes:

North Korean "revolutionary opera" like this one transforms Korean folk tales into powerful political propaganda.

> Traditional music is similar to that of Japan and China, with an emphasis on strings. The two main forms are the stately *chongak* and the folksier *minsogak*. Among the folk dances

are drum dances (*mugo*—a hectic, lively court dance where the participants wear drums around their necks), mask dances (*talchum*), monk dances (*seungmu*) and spirit-cleansing dances (*salpuri*).[16]

However, like other forms of culture, music is also used for political purposes. For example, "revolutionary operas," often taken from traditional Korean operas, turn traditional Korean folk stories into revolutionary themes. Similarly, many musical compositions are hymns that praise North Korea's leaders, with titles such as "We Sing of His Benevolent Love" and "Long Life and Good Health to the Leader."

A recent interview of North Korean singers who had defected from North Korea reveals the depth of government influence over the arts there. In the interview, Choi Hee-Soon, a member of T'ongil Ye Sul Dan, a performing arts group made up of North Korean defectors, explained, "In North Korea, there is no individual expression.... There is no such thing as private words or emotion."[17] Another member of the group added, "If I were to play in North Korea, it would be only to sing and to celebrate the birthdays of Kim Il-sung or Kim Jong-il or for collectively-held events."[18]

SPORTS

Traditional Korean sports are limited primarily to martial arts, archery, and a Korean version of wrestling similar to Japanese sumo wrestling, called *ssirum*. Perhaps the most famous Korean martial art is tae kwon do, which involves person-to-person combat without weapons and short bursts of physical contact. Various sports, however, are pursued in modern North Korea, and despite its economic troubles, the North Korean government has encouraged and funded athletic achievement, often as a means to promote the country and its government.

One of the most popular modern sports in North Korea is gymnastics. Mass gymnastic displays, performed by tens of thousands of North Koreans in uniform, often are organized for special events, such as the birthdays of Kim Il Sung or Kim Jong Il or when foreign dignitaries are visiting.

North Korean athletes also have been good enough to win at international competitions. For example, North Korea sent its athletes to the 1996 Summer Olympics held in the United

States at Atlanta, Georgia, where North Korean Kye Sun Hui won a gold medal in women's judo. In addition, North Koreans won medals in boxing, wrestling, and weight lifting in the 1976 and 1980 Summer Olympics. Also in one of the most famous North Korean athletic feats, North Korean soccer players beat the powerful Italian soccer team and reached the quarter finals of the 1966 World Cup.

North and South Korean athletes marched together during the opening ceremonies of the Fourteenth Asian Games held in 2002 in Pusan, South Korea.

In 2002, North Korean athletes traveled to South Korea's port city of Pusan to participate in the Fourteenth Asian Games, a prestigious Asian sports competition with athletes from forty-four Asian countries. Indeed, in a show of Korean unity in Pusan, North Koreans marched with and wore the same uniforms as South Korean athletes, in an emotional opening ceremony. In 2003, North Korea won two medals in the Fifth Winter Asian Games held in Aomori Prefecture, Japan—a silver medal in women's three-thousand-meter short-truck speed skating relay and a bronze medal in women's five-hundred-meter short-truck speed skating.

Sports stadiums in P'yongyang, North Korea, include the P'yongyang Indoor Stadium, which offers 20,000 seats in four floors; the May Day Stadium, a huge facility with eight floors, 150,000 seats, a swimming pool, and saunas; and Kim Il Sung Stadium, a stadium that was enlarged to 100,000 seats to celebrate the seventieth birthday of Kim Il Sung.

EDUCATION

Like culture, the education system in North Korea is based largely on concepts promoted by the government, such as

KIM IL SUNG UNIVERSITY

Kim Il Sung University, North Korea's most important university, was founded on October 12, 1946, the year following Korea's liberation from Japanese rule, in P'yongyang. It was named after North Korean leader, Kim Il Sung, who spoke at the school on more than five hundred occasions about its main mission—to perform applied scientific research and engineering to help North Korea achieve its civilian and military goals.

Today, the university has grown significantly since its formation and is considered the home of *Juche* teaching and a model for other universities. It has fourteen faculties of social and natural sciences, including economics, history, mathematics, philosophy, and biology and other institutes devoted to cell engineering, atomic energy, and computer related areas. It also employs more than twelve hundred persons with academic degrees as well as other academicians, professors, doctors, teachers, and scholars. Each year the university graduates tens of thousands of North Koreans, many of whom eventually play major roles in North Korea's political, scientific, educational, cultural, and military sectors.

Students crowd the campus of Kim Il Sung University in P'yongyang.

Juche ideas. It was modeled on the Soviet Union's education system. By 1975, North Korea claimed to have established a compulsory eleven-year education requirement for all North Koreans, which by the 1990s included one year of preschool education, four years of primary school for ages six to nine, and six years of senior middle school for ages ten to fifteen. This compulsory education is paid for by the government.

Subjects taught in North Korean schools during the 1990s included academic courses, such as mathematics, science and technology, and Korean language; courses in music, art, and physical education; and political courses with names such as "Communist Morality," the "Great Kim Il Sung," and "Communist Party Policy." However, even nonpolitical subjects are infused with political ideas. For example, language textbooks have titles such as *Love of Our Father* and *We Pray for "Our Master"* (references to Kim Il Sung). Also, the writings of Kim Il Sung are given great authority and studied in North Korean schools.

North Korea also has colleges, universities, medical schools, military academies, and various two- or three-year technical schools that offer higher education. The most prestigious university in North Korea is Kim Il Sung University, located in P'yongyang, which provides bachelor's, master's, and doctoral degrees. The criteria for admission include good grades, but admission is based mostly on political considerations, such as status within the group of government elites.

However, education in North Korea is not limited to formal instruction; rather, North Koreans are encouraged by the government to learn concepts promoted by the government in all activities. For example, the government encourages families to teach their children values such as frugality, courtesy, and dedication to social and political goals. Similarly, people are urged to participate in various social groups, cultural events, and extracurricular activities that exist for the purpose of teaching political and cultural values.

HEALTH CARE

Like its education system, North Korea's health-care system was modeled on that of the Soviet Union system. In this system, health care is both managed and funded by the state. Numerous hospitals were built, preventative medicine was emphasized, and the health and longevity of the North Korean population dramatically improved during the first three decades of Kim Il Sung's rule.

One unique aspect of North Korean health care is the development of traditional herbal medicine, known as *Tongui-hak,* or Eastern Medicine. This branch of medicine relies on curative herbs, which are given orally or burned on the skin, as well as acupuncture, which uses needles to puncture the body at specific points to induce healing. Pharmacies in North Korea distribute herbal-medicine products, including items such as ginseng (*insam*) and a metabolism activator (*tonghae chongsimhwan*) made from herbs, as well as other products collected from along the country's eastern shores. North Koreans claim that herbal medicines are superior to Western medicines because they are more natural and have few dangerous side effects. However, Western medicines are also used to treat the ailments of North Koreans.

Since the economic downturn and food crisis that began in the 1990s, however, the health of the North Korean people is known to have declined. Mass starvation and malnourishment have been documented. Yet because the North Korean government keeps much of this information secret, the true picture of health and health care in North Korea today is uncertain.

ETHNICITY AND LANGUAGE

Yet another aspect of North Korea's culture is its high degree of ethnic and racial homogeneity; indeed, most Koreans, in both North and South, are descended from the same ancestors and speak a similar Korean language. Although Koreans borrowed many cultural elements from neighboring countries such as China and Japan, Koreans are easily distinguishable from these other Asian populations. Koreans were descended from migratory groups who traveled to the Korea Peninsula from Siberia, Manchuria, and Central Asia several thousands of years ago. Although both China and Japan have colonized Koreans, neither was able to eradicate the ethnic, cultural, and linguistic distinctiveness of Koreans.

The Korean language, according to most linguists, originated in northern Asia and is a combination of influences from the Mongol, Turkic, Finnish, Hungarian, and Tungusic (Chinese Manchu) languages. Also, although no clear connection has been shown, there is a striking similarity between Ko-

TRADITIONAL KOREAN FOOD

Traditional Korean food begins with rice, either plain or cooked with other grains, usually accompanied by spicy side dishes. Various other dishes, also often heavily flavored with herbs and spices, are then placed in the middle of the table and shared by everyone. These dishes are often made from green vegetables, seafood, and (less frequently) from poultry, pork, or beef. Bean sprouts and bean curd, or tofu, also are popular ingredients. Like many other Asian cultures, North Koreans use chopsticks, spoons, and rice bowls.

The most striking characteristic of Korean food is how hot and spicy it is, usually relying on red pepper and garlic as the key ingredients. For example, a side dish that is served with everything and that is considered an essential element of any Korean meal is kimchi, a very spicy dish made from cabbage and sometimes other vegetables that are pickled with hot red peppers, garlic, and other seasonings. Another very popular Korean dish is *bulgogi,* made from strips of beef that are first marinated in a spicy mixture of soy sauce, sesame seeds, garlic, green onions, hot red peppers, and other seasonings, and then grilled.

rean and Japanese. Both languages employ similar grammatical structures and both use "polite" or more formal speech to address persons of superior rank, with various other nuances depending on the relationships involved. For example, as explained in the Library of Congress study, "in Korean, the imperative 'go' can be rendered *kara* for speaking to an inferior or a child, *kage* to an adult inferior, *kao* or *kaseyo* to a superior, and *kusipsio* to a person of still higher rank." [19] These distinctions are very subtle, in both Korean and Japanese, but generally one would use formal language when meeting someone for the first time or in addressing elders and use more informal terms with friends and children.

Korean can be written using either a mixture of Chinese characters (called *hancha*) and a native Korean alphabet known as *han'gul,* or by using *han'gul* alone. *Han'gul* was developed in about 1446 during the reign of King Sejong, one of ancient Korea's most progressive and most beloved monarchs. Until then, Koreans could only use Chinese characters for literary purposes, which meant that anyone wanting to write had to learn a new and complex grammar system very different from the Korean spoken language.

The items in this North Korean department store are sold exclusively to party members and tourists. The ability to purchase certain goods is largely determined by social status.

Nevertheless, due to the great cultural influence that China has had on Koreans throughout history, the Korean language still uses a large number of words borrowed from the Chinese language. Often, Koreans have two words that mean the same thing, one a more formal Chinese-based word and the other a native Korean word. Koreans decide which word to use depending on the degree of formality required.

In modern North Korea, the government has sought to eliminate the use of these Chinese words as well as the use of

Chinese *hancha* characters in writing. Official publications, for example, such as the monthly KWP journal, are printed in *han'gul.* In addition, unlike South Koreans who speak a dialect from Seoul, the capital city of South Korea, North Koreans speak a version of the Korean language that uses the regional dialect of North Korea's capital city, P'yongyang, as the standard. North Koreans consider their language to be the "Cultured Language," or *munhwa,* and Kim Il Sung wrote papers which defined the country's policies concerning *munhwa.* In addition, Kim Il Sung asked North Koreans to use a special, honorific language toward himself and his family.

CLASS STRUCTURE AND WORK

Despite the promises of equality contained in Communist political ideals, modern North Korea has a clearly defined social and class structure reminiscent of ancient Korea. Unlike ancient Korea, however, the social strata of contemporary North Korea are completely determined by the state, since it is the only source of resources or wealth. North Korea's leader, Kim Jong Il, for example, is reported to live like a king, in grand houses with every luxury available. Next in line is a small group of ruling elite within the KWP, who are closely tied to Kim Jong Il and who have a relatively high standard of living and access to consumer goods not available to ordinary North Koreans. Lower-echelon KWP members form the next social group. These individuals, although perhaps limited in their access to food and goods, at least have more opportunities for education and advancement than nonmembers.

At the bottom of North Korea's social rung are ordinary workers. Traditionally, most ordinary people worked as farmers, but this changed after the country's industrialization. In the late 1980s, for example, the North Korean government classified its labor force into four categories: "workers" employed at state-owned businesses and who constituted more than half of the country's labor force; "farmers" who worked on agricultural collectives; "officials" who performed non-manual labor and included occupations such as teachers and health-care workers; and workers employed in "cooperative industrial units," which can best be described as North Korea's tiny private-sector businesses.

Social status determines access to food and other essential goods. For example, food is strictly rationed in North Korea, with different worker categories receiving unequal quantities and qualities of food. The same is true of other necessities and consumer goods; North Korea has some department stores, but they are limited to KWP members and foreigners. Similarly, one's access to housing in North Korea depends on class status, and ordinary workers and farmers typically live in multiunit dwellings of no more than one or two rooms.

Also, family background and political history, such as participation in the Korean War, can improve social status and access to necessities and opportunities in North Korea. Conversely, those descended from families who collaborated with the Japanese during Korea's colonial era are discriminated against. Physically disabled persons also appear to be social outcasts in North Korea.

In modern North Korea, therefore, life and culture are strictly controlled by the state, and only those affiliated with or approved of by the government have any chance of living well.

North Korea
in Distress

Recent decades have brought grim developments and huge challenges for North Korea. Events such as the collapse of the Soviet Union, the death of Kim Il Sung, and a famine have left North Korea's economy in a downward spiral, its people starving, and its place in the world insecure. Making matters worse, the North Korean regime (now headed by Kim's son, Kim Jong Il) has responded to the country's crisis by continuing Kim Il Sung's failed policies and further emphasizing the need for military strength. As part of this plan, North Korea has developed nuclear and other weapons of mass destruction, an action that today places North Korea on a collision course with the United States and other countries concerned about the spread of such weapons.

THE COLLAPSE OF COMMUNISM

The first serious blow to North Korea came in the late 1980s when most of the world's Communist countries, eventually including the Soviet Union, abandoned communism as a political and economic system. The process began in 1985, when Mikhail Gorbachev became premier of the Soviet Union and relaxed government restrictions on political dissent and economic activity. Soon thereafter, people in other Communist countries, such as Poland, East Germany, Czechoslovakia, Bulgaria, Romania, and Hungary, demanded similar democratic and economic reforms. Eventually these Communist governments collapsed, and in 1991, the Soviet Union finally did as well.

North Korea, like China, did not abandon communism, but the Soviet collapse nevertheless caused serious problems for North Korea because it ended the Soviet aid North Korea needed to survive. In addition, the collapse of other Communist countries eliminated the traditional markets for North

Korea's goods and exports, further reducing the country's income. On top of these problems, North Korea now had to pay in cash at world market prices for essential goods such as oil, industrial equipment, and raw materials. (In the past, North Korea had obtained these goods from the Soviets in exchange for generous trade credits.) By December 1993, North Korea publicly acknowledged the tremendous blow to its economy caused by the breakup of the Soviet Union, indicating in an official statement that the economy was in a "grave situation" and suffering "grim trials."[20]

North Korea's plight worsened when its other supporter, China, was unable to replace the lost Soviet aid. China was working to restructure its own economy and had already begun decreasing its support for North Korea. Under the leadership of Deng Xiaoping, China reformed its economy and opened it to trade with the United States and the West. In addition, in 1992, China formally recognized South Korea and began trading with the North Korean enemy. These reforms integrated China into the world capitalist economy, but at the same time weakened trade with North Korea just when it was most needed.

NORTH KOREA'S FAMINE AND ECONOMIC DECLINE

North Korea's loss of economic support was followed by natural disasters that destroyed harvests and devastated the nation's agricultural production. By the end of the century, North Korea was barely surviving.

North Korea's food supply, already weakened by blows to the country's economy, seriously deteriorated in 1995 and 1996, when the country experienced a number of devastating floods. The heavy rains and flooding destroyed crops and washed away soil in many growing areas. Decreases in fertilizer production further decreased agricultural yields in 1996. The rains were followed by a serious drought and tidal waves along North Korea's western coast. These disasters damaged farmland even more.

The floods and drought, and resulting food shortages, caused homelessness, famine, and mass starvation in North Korea. The government's distribution of food to rural areas was cut in half or less in 1996, and it sometimes stopped completely. As a result, North Koreans were forced to eat grass, roots, tree bark, and

THE FAMINE IN NORTH KOREA

North Koreans have not had enough food since the early 1990s, when the cutoff of Soviet aid left North Korea without resources to buy food and natural disasters destroyed the country's agricultural industry. The famine is causing widespread malnutrition and starvation. Estimates vary, but it is clear that hundreds of thousands of North Koreans have died of malnutrition and related diseases since the mid-1990s. Tens of thousands more have fled to neighboring countries such as China to escape the hunger. Even North Korea admits that up to 45 percent of its children under five are chronically malnourished.

The government provides food rations but the rations are not equally distributed. Associates of Kim Jong Il receive the most food, while ordinary people receive very little or none. Typical food rations in June 2002 provided about half the minimum recommended level of nutrition necessary for a healthy adult. Those who can afford it buy supplemental food at illegal farmers' markets that have sprung up to meet the demand for food. To survive, those who cannot buy extra food are quitting school or jobs to scrounge for wild food.

The United Nations has provided massive food aid to North Korea since the mid-1990s. The food aid continued in 2002 and 2003, but the UN's World Food Program (WFP), the primary provider of food to the country, experienced a drop in contributions from donating countries. Japan and the United States completely cut off their contributions to the WFP in 2002 because of North Korea's nuclear weapons issues and tough political stance. On February 25, 2003, the United States announced that it will resume shipments of food aid to North Korea, but said it would cut donations in 2003 by between 35 and 75 percent from the previous year's totals. China also provides food assistance to North Korea, separately from the WFP program.

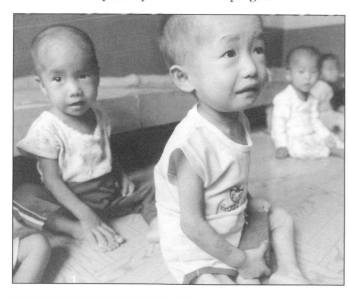

Recent famines in North Korea have caused widespread malnutrition and starvation.

similar items to try to survive. Illegal farmers' markets sprang up around the country, and some North Koreans began to flee across the border to China to escape North Korea's economic troubles. Nevertheless, many people, especially children, simply died as a result of the lack of food. Indeed, estimates have run as high as 2 million deaths from starvation and related causes since the start of the crisis—close to one-tenth of North Korea's population. In a speech given on December 7, 1996, even Kim Jong Il admitted, "the food problem is creating a state of anarchy." [21]

The situation became so serious that North Korea, whose main ideal was self-reliance, was forced to ask the world for help. Its first request came in 1995, when it asked the UN for nearly $500 million in flood relief, fuel, and medical assistance. Since then, North Korea has depended on massive amounts of UN food aid to feed its people. However, many experts suggest that most of the food sent to North Korea is distributed to government officials who are loyal to Kim Jong Il, with very little ending up in the hands of hungry citizens.

During the 1990s, natural and economic disasters caused fuel shortages in North Korea. As a result, people were forced to travel on foot or by bicycle.

Despite the UN's assistance, North Korea's economy continued to collapse. The lack of fuel caused factories to close and disabled most forms of modern transportation, such as trains and buses, reducing people to traveling in oxcarts and on bicycles. This lack of fuel also damaged food production even more, because factories were not producing necessary fertilizer and because food that was produced could not be properly distributed. In addition, electrical blackouts became common, and many offices and homes could not be heated, even during North Korea's bitterly cold winters. Even the state-run television station was occasionally forced off the air due to lack of power to run its transmitters. In 1997, the International Monetary Fund, after a visit to North Korea, reported that the country's economy had declined significantly, with total industrial and agricultural output only half of what it was five years earlier. By the year 2000, many observers were predicting that the country would soon collapse.

THE DEATH OF KIM IL SUNG

On July 8, 1994, in the middle of North Korea's economic crises, its leader, Kim Il Sung, died of a heart attack. He was replaced by his son, Kim Jong Il, who was designated as his father's successor years before. With his father's death, Kim Jong Il inherited a country with many critical problems and on the verge of economic collapse.

Kim Jong Il clearly needed to reform North Korea's economy, but this placed him in a terrible dilemma—if he opened North Korea to the world for economic reform, it could threaten his regime and his ability to control the North Korean population. The events in the Soviet Union and Eastern European countries showed that similar reforms and openness could quickly topple governments. As a result, Kim Jong Il continued his father's strategy of limited economic reform, tried to raise cash and survive by any means possible, and strengthened the military to fend off threats to his regime.

KIM JONG IL'S TENTATIVE ECONOMIC REFORMS

Kim Jong Il has cautiously experimented with economic reforms similar to those implemented by China in its economic modernization program. Even before Kim Jong Il had succeeded his father, in 1984, North Korea enacted its first Joint Venture Law to promote foreign investments in its economy.

Later, in 1992, North Korea enacted three sets of new laws to make it easier for foreign companies to do business in and with North Korea. North Korea also sought technical assistance from the UN Committee for Trade and Development to help it develop an international trade strategy and improve its knowledge in the areas of foreign trade, exports, and free economic and export zones.

Finally, in July 2002, North Korea undertook what many believe could be a very significant step in moving from a Communist economy to a free-market economy. This step involved moving wages and prices, which had long been dictated by the government, closer to market levels. Simultaneously, the government began phasing out its controls over the economy, such as state subsidies for industries and ration coupons that North Koreans use to pay for food, clothing, and other staples. If successful, this reform could dramatically change North Korea's economy from one that is dictated by the state to one that depends on market demands, allowing the country eventually to integrate into the world economy.

All of these actions are similar to the changes that China pursued in its economic modernization program, but so far the results have been disappointing for North Korea. The foreign investment initiatives have mostly encouraged only a few South Koreans and Japanese Koreans to invest in North Korea; Western companies have avoided ventures with North Korea due to the high risks involved in investing in an unstable country. Other North Korean economic efforts have been extremely tentative and have revealed the country's inflexibility, lack of knowledge, and inability to respond to economic challenges. North Korea's most recent reform of its wage and price structure is too new for outsiders to effectively assess its potential or results.

Finally, despite attempted reforms, an underlying problem in North Korea's economy is the country's huge foreign debt and lack of a good credit rating—North Korea cannot hope to increase its exports without huge investments in high-tech equipment and plants, and that is not possible without borrowing money and interacting with outsiders.

NEGOTIATING FOR SURVIVAL

As part of his survival strategy, Kim Jong Il has attempted to improve North Korea's relationships with other countries. Improved

FAMILY REUNIONS

Korea's division at the end of World War II and the hostilities created by the Korean War have left many Korean families separated for more than fifty years, with some family members living in North Korea and others remaining in South Korea. The historic summit between North Korean leader Kim Jong Il and South Korean president Kim Dae Jung in June 2000 paved the way for some of these family members to finally reunite, if only briefly, with their long-lost relatives. An October 11, 2002, article in *Current Events* magazine titled "Homecoming: Family Reunions Spark Hopes for a United Korea" described some of the poignant moments at one of the first of these family reunions:

> When South Korean Kim Hae-on, 93, touched the wrinkled hands of his wife for the first time in 50 years, he said, "Can you recognize me? You're alive. Thank you. I've waited for this day." His wife wept
>
> South Korean sisters Lee Jin-ock and Lee Jin-geum broke down when they saw their 82 year-old father. For years, the sisters held memorial services for their father, assuming he had died when he went out shopping during the war and never returned.
>
> Though she'd been born blind, Kim Kunrye, a 67-year-old South Korean, could still recognize the voice of her older brother, Kim Hak Rye, after five decades.

When the three-day visits ended, family members found it very difficult to say good-bye because they knew they might never see each other again.

Korean family members divided by the border weep during a 2002 reunion. Many families have been separated since the country's division at the end of World War II.

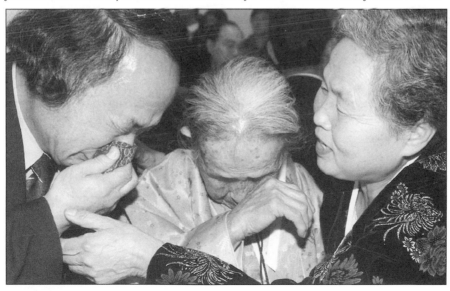

relations with longtime adversaries such as the United States, South Korea, and Japan could help the country get loans from the international community through sources such as the World Bank and the International Monetary Fund. Kim Jong Il has also used contacts with other countries to negotiate for economic aid and security guarantees.

In 1994, for example, Kim Jong Il completed negotiations that his father began with the United States on North Korea's nuclear weapons program. By the late 1990s, North Korea openly negotiated for food assistance. It agreed to participate in peace talks with the United States and South Korea and reduce military tensions on the Korea Peninsula in exchange for humanitarian aid. In 1997 North Korea agreed to four-way peace talks with the United States, South Korea, and China, first demanding food aid as a concession for its participation. In 1998, when the United States discovered what appeared to be a secret underground nuclear weapons facility in North Korea, Kim Jong Il agreed to permit inspections of the site, again in exchange for aid.

Since 1999, North Korea has made efforts to reestablish or strengthen relationships with China, Russia, and Japan and has participated in a historic summit meeting with South Korean president Kim Dae Jung. These contacts have produced many benefits for North Korea. For example, South Korea paid Kim Jong Il $200 million to attend the 2000 summit, which then resulted in additional aid and economic ventures and inspired the United States to partially lift U.S. trade sanctions against the country. Also, after the summit, South Korea supported North Korea's bid to join the Asian Regional Forum, a regional security organization, and the Asian Development Bank, an international financial organization.

Similarly, another historic summit in 2002 provided North Korea with economic assistance when Kim Jong Il met with Japan's prime minister, Junichiro Koizumi. These talks resulted in an admission by North Korea that it had abducted eleven Japanese citizens during the Cold War to act as language instructors, an apology from Japan for its colonization and wartime conduct in Korea, and a package of billions of dollars of aid to North Korea.

NORTH KOREA'S MISSILE SALES

North Korea, desperate for cash, also began to export anything it could to bring in income. Its most successful export became

NORTH KOREA'S CHEMICAL AND BIOLOGICAL WEAPONS

In addition to its nuclear weapons and missile programs, the United States believes North Korea also has developed large stocks of chemical and biological weapons. For example, U.S. experts believe that North Korea has a national-level biological weapons program that has produced biological weapons using smallpox, cholera, yellow fever, typhus, and other viruses. In addition, the United States thinks North Korea has already developed the capacity to produce large amounts of chemical weapons, including mustard, phosgene, and sarin. A defense paper published by the South Korean government, for example, has concluded that North Korea has a minimum of twenty-five hundred tons of these lethal chemicals.

ballistic missiles and missile technology, which it sold to controversial countries such as Iran, Syria, Egypt, and Pakistan. According to the U.S. State Department, North Korea earned close to a billion dollars in missile sales over the last decade, making it the biggest missile exporter in the world. These missile sales continue today; as recently as 2002, for example, the United States intercepted a North Korean ship delivering missiles to Yemen.

Although North Korea began developing its missile technology in the late 1980s, the world did not take notice until August 1998, when North Korea launched a medium-range, multistage Taepo-Dong I missile across Japan and into the Pacific Ocean. In North Korea, this test launch was lauded as an example of the country's strength. To the rest of the world, however, the missile firing was seen as a threatening act, proving that North Korea could attack South Korea, U.S. forces stationed there, and Japan with either conventional or nuclear/chemical/biological weapons.

Following the test, the United States unsuccessfully negotiated with North Korea for an agreement to end its missile development. Instead, North Korea voluntarily halted further missile tests for an unspecified period in September 1999, and in response, the United States indicated it might be willing to ease U.S. economic sanctions that prohibited most exports and imports to and from North Korea. Since then, North Korea extended its moratorium on missile testing. However, in the absence of an agreement banning North Korea's missile program, the country continued to develop short-, medium-, and long-range missiles. It also continued to sell this missile technology in earnest to other countries.

These missile exports have provided much-needed income and have given North Korea bargaining leverage with the United States. North Korea, for example, has offered to halt missile exports in exchange for economic concessions from the United States, including, for example, compensation payments of $500 million per year for the loss of missile sales. The proliferation of missiles and technology, however, has already created instability in both Asia and the Middle East, as missile sales give other dangerous countries the ability to threaten their neighbors and pose the risk of regional arms races in those areas.

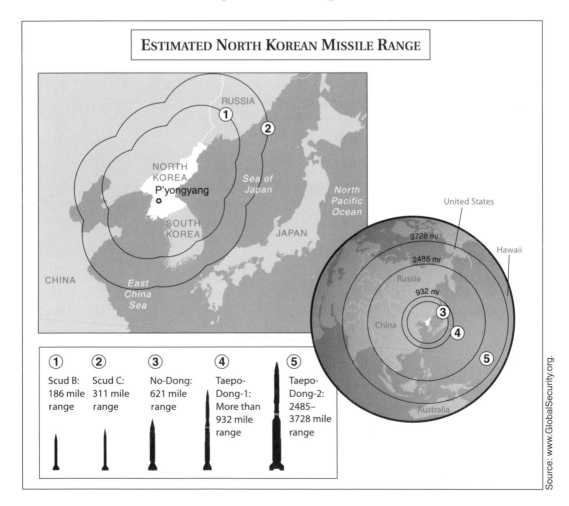

ESTIMATED NORTH KOREAN MISSILE RANGE

① Scud B: 186 mile range ② Scud C: 311 mile range ③ No-Dong: 621 mile range ④ Taepo-Dong-1: More than 932 mile range ⑤ Taepo-Dong-2: 2485–3728 mile range

According to U.S. intelligence information, North Korea now has long-range missiles that can reach the continental United States. If North Korea decides to sell this long-range missile technology, the United States will be especially concerned, because it will give other anti-American countries the ability to strike the United States.

NORTH KOREA'S NUCLEAR WEAPONS PROGRAM

North Korea's missile program is part of a concerted effort by Kim Jong Il to improve the country's military strength and readiness. Indeed, most experts believe that North Korea, under Kim Jong Il, is now ruled by military rather than political leaders, a development that the United States and many other countries are wary of since it might make the already desperate country more prone to attack its neighbors. Even more frightening, a large part of Kim Jong Il's military program, in addition to missile development, has focused on the development of nuclear, chemical, and biological weapons. This has made North Korea a highly volatile actor in the international arena and has created great instability for its Asian neighbors.

North Korea's experiments with nuclear power began as early as 1962, but in 1985 North Korea was pressured by other countries into signing the Nuclear Non-Proliferation Treaty (NPT), the main international treaty aimed at stopping the spread of nuclear weapons. However, North Korea did not agree at this time to allow international inspections of its nuclear facilities to ensure it was complying with the NPT. Instead, North Korea continued its nuclear program by constructing a nuclear reactor capable of producing plutonium for nuclear weapons, and by beginning construction of an additional, larger reactor.

By 1989, the United States became alarmed about North Korea's nuclear activities. U.S. spy satellites detected evidence of yet another nuclear reactor as well as a building that looked like a nuclear reprocessing facility—that is, a facility that can extract plutonium from nuclear reactor fuel for use in nuclear weapons. With this nuclear reprocessing plant, experts predicted North Korea could make up to forty nuclear bombs per year.

North Korea's nuclear activities finally sparked an international crisis in 1992, after North Korea was finally pressured to agree to inspections of nuclear facilities. Inspections by the International Atomic Energy Agency (IAEA), however, discovered that North Korea had produced more plutonium than it admitted, and North Korea halted inspections and threatened war if inspections or sanctions were forced upon it. In April 1993, they proposed bilateral negotiations with the United States to end the crisis. Talks between the two countries resulted in the 1994 Framework Agreement, in which North Korea agreed to freeze its nuclear weapons development program in exchange for aid.

Some experts predicted that the 1994 agreement would not stop North Korea from developing nuclear weapons in the future. Because its nuclear facilities had not been destroyed, these experts said North Korea could simply restart its nuclear program. In addition, they suggested that North Korea probably already had extracted enough plutonium from its nuclear reactors to build at least two nuclear bombs. These predictions soon proved correct.

THE 2002 NUCLEAR WEAPONS CRISIS

The September 11, 2001, terrorist attacks prompted the United States to take a more critical view of countries that seek nuclear and other weapons of mass destruction. As part of this post–September 11 policy, U.S. president George W. Bush announced in his January 2002 State of the Union address that the United States would stop governments such as North Korea from threatening other countries with weapons of mass destruction. In this speech, Bush named three countries that he said were part of an "axis of evil" that was arming to threaten the peace of the world—Iraq, Iran, and North Korea. "By seeking weapons of mass destruction," Bush said, "these regimes pose a grave and growing danger. They could provide these arms to terrorists, giving them the means to match their hatred. They could attack our allies or attempt to blackmail the United States." [22]

Thereafter, after many months of hostilities, U.S. and North Korean negotiators agreed to meet in October 2002. During these talks, North Korea admitted that it was, once again, developing nuclear weapons, this time with a program that uses uranium instead of plutonium for making nuclear weapons. In addition, North Korea suggested that it had more powerful weapons as well, a statement that U.S. officials interpreted to mean that North Korea has other types of weapons of mass destruction, such as chemical and biological weapons. The

United States said that North Korea's actions placed it in violation of its promises not to develop nuclear weapons, including the 1994 Framework Agreement.

For its part, North Korea justified its decision to develop nuclear weapons by claiming it needed them to defend itself against the United States. For example, the North Korean state-run radio broadcasted a statement that its government "has come to have nuclear and other strong military weapons due to nuclear threats by U.S. imperialists."[23] Later, North Korea downplayed this statement and proposed a nonaggression treaty with the United States as the solution to the crisis.

When the United States refused to negotiate such a treaty with North Korea and engineered the cutoff of fuel promised to the country under the 1994 agreement, North Korea responded with a number of provocative statements and actions that escalated the crisis. For example, it dismantled surveillance cameras that were installed to monitor the 1994

Kim Jong Il's (center) program to develop nuclear weapons prompted U.S. president George W. Bush to condemn North Korea as a tremendous threat to global security.

agreement, threatened to reopen its plutonium reprocessing plant, and ordered IAEA inspectors to leave the country. In January 2003, North Korea pulled out of the Nuclear Non-Proliferation Treaty. Later, North Korea announced it had reactivated its plutonium nuclear facilities, sent its fighter jets to intercept an unarmed U.S. spy plane, and test fired two anti-ship missiles into the Sea of Japan.

North Korea also threatened war if the United States made a preemptive strike on its nuclear facilities and warned it would abandon its commitment to the 1953 armistice that ended the Korean War. In April 2003, talks finally began between North Korea, the United States, and China, but these were suspended after North Korea announced it already had nuclear weapons. Later, North Korea said it had produced enough plutonium to make six more bombs and was moving to produce them. As of early 2004, the crisis had not been resolved.

The 2002–2003 nuclear crisis appeared to many to be yet another example of North Korea's efforts to extort aid and security from the United States and South Korea. Others say that Kim Jong Il has no intention of negotiating away his nuclear weapons because he believes he needs nuclear weapons to protect his country from being attacked or his regime from being overthrown by the United States or other countries. Still others, however, worry that North Korea's pursuit of nuclear weapons might be for offensive purposes, to carry out its historical goal of forcing a reunification with South Korea under Communist rule. Regardless of Kim Jong Il's motivation, what does seem clear is that North Korea is committed to building nuclear weapons, a scenario the United States deems completely unacceptable.

FACTS ABOUT
NORTH KOREA

GEOGRAPHY

Location: Eastern Asia, northern half of the Korea Peninsula bordering the Korea Bay (Yellow Sea) and the Sea of Japan, between China and South Korea

Area total: 46,540 square miles; land: 46,490 square miles; water: 50 square miles

Area comparative: Slightly smaller than Mississippi

Bordering countries: China, South Korea, Russia

Coastline: 1,547 miles on the Sea of Japan in the east and the Yellow Sea in the west

Climate: Temperate, with rainfall concentrated in summer

Terrain: Mostly hills and mountains separated by deep, narrow valleys; coastal plains wide in west, discontinuous in east

Natural resources: Coal, lead, tungsten, zinc, graphite, magnesite, iron ore, copper, gold, pyrites, salt, fluorspar

Land use: Arable land, 14%; permanent crops, 2%; permanent pastures, 0%; forests and woodlands, 61%; other, 23%; (1993 estimate)

Natural hazards: Late-spring droughts often followed by severe flooding; occasional typhoons during the early fall

Environmental issues: Localized air pollution attributable to inadequate industrial controls; water pollution; inadequate supplies of potable water

PEOPLE

Population: 21,386,109 (July 1999 estimate)

Age structure: 0–14 years, 26% (male 2,800,748; female 2,666,207); 15–64 years, 68% (male 7,143,969; female 7,447,147); 65 years and over, 6% (male 412,161; female 915,877) (1999 estimate)

Population growth rate: 1.45% (1999 estimate)

Birth rate: 21.37 births/1,000 population (1999 estimate)

Death rate: 6.92 deaths/1,000 population (1999 estimate)

Infant mortality rate: 25.52 deaths/1,000 live births (1999 estimate)

Life expectancy: Total population, 70.07 years; male, 67.41 years; female, 72.86 years (1999 estimate)

Fertility rate: 2.3 children born/woman (1999 estimate)

Ethnic groups: Racially homogeneous; there is a small Chinese community and there are a few ethnic Japanese

Religions: Buddhism and Confucianism, some Christianity and Tonghak; note, however, that religious activities are now almost nonexistent

Language: Korean

Literacy rate for those age 15 and over: Total population, 99%; male, 99%; female, 99% (1990 estimate)

GOVERNMENT

Country name: Democratic People's Republic of Korea (DPRK) or North Korea

Form of government: Communist state; one-man dictatorship

Capital: P'yongyang

Administrative divisions: 9 provinces and 3 special cities

National holiday: Foundation Day, September 9 (1948)(the date the country was founded); National Liberation Day, August 15 (1945)(the date of independence from the Japanese)

Constitution: Adopted 1948; completely revised December 27, 1972; revised again in April 1992 and September 1998

Legal system: Based on German civil law system with Japanese influences and Communist legal theory; no judicial review of legislative acts

Suffrage: 17 years of age; universal

Executive branch: After President Kim Il Sung died in 1994, his son Kim Jong Il became North Korea's chief of state; in September 1998, Kim Jong Il was reelected chairman of the National Defense Commission, a position accorded the nation's "highest administrative authority"; Kim Young-nam was named president of the Supreme People's Assembly Presidium and given the responsibility of representing the state and receiving diplomatic credentials.

Legislative branch: Unicameral Supreme People's Assembly, or *Ch'oego Inmin Hoeui* (687 seats; members elected by popular vote to serve five-year terms); the KWP approves a single list of candidates who are elected without opposition; minor parties hold a few seats

Judicial branch: Central Court; judges are elected by the Supreme People's Assembly

Political parties: Major party, Korean Workers' Party (KWP); Korean Social Democratic Party; Chondoist Chongu Party

Flag: Three horizontal bands of blue (top), red (triple width), and blue; the red band is edged in white; on the hoist side of the red band is a white disk containing a red five-pointed star

ECONOMY

Gross domestic product (GDP): $21.8 billion (1998 estimate); real growth, 5%, (1998 estimate); GDP per capita, $1,000 (1998 estimate); GDP composition, agriculture 25%, industry 60%, services 15% (1995 estimate)

Labor force: 9.615 million

Industries: Military products (machine building, electric power); chemicals; mining (coal, iron ore, magnesite, graphite, copper, zinc, lead, and precious metals); metallurgy; textiles, food processing

Agriculture products: Rice, corn, potatoes, soybeans, pulses; cattle, pigs, pork, eggs

Exports: $743 million (1997 estimate)

Imports: $1.83 billion (1997 estimate)

Debt: $12 billion (1996 estimate)

Economic aid: An estimated $200 million to $300 million in humanitarian aid from the United States, South Korea, Japan, and the European Union in 1997

Currency: 1 North Korean won (Wn) = 100 chon

NOTES

CHAPTER 1: LAND IN THE MOUNTAINS

1. Quoted in Andrea Matles Savada, ed., *North Korea, a Country Study.* Washington, DC: Government Printing Office, 1994, p. 51.

2. Quoted in Savada, *North Korea, a Country Study,* p. 57.

3. Quoted in Savada, *North Korea, a Country Study.* p. 144.

CHAPTER 2: KOREA'S RICH HISTORY

4. Geoff Simons, *Korea: The Search for Sovereignty.* New York: St. Martin's Press, 1995, p. 131.

5. Korean Overseas Information Service, *Focus on Korea: Korean History.* Seoul, Republic of Korea: Seoul International, 1986, p. 98.

6. Quoted in Savada, *North Korea, a Country Study.* p. 29.

7. Bruce Cumings, *Korea's Place in the Sun.* New York: W.W. Norton, 1997, p. 10.

CHAPTER 3: COMMUNIST NORTH KOREA

8. Don Oberdorfer, *The Two Koreas.* Canada: Basic Books, 2001, p. 20.

9. Quoted in Chuck Downs, *Over the Line, North Korea's Negotiating Strategy.* Washington, DC: AIE Press, 1999, p. 165.

CHAPTER 4: NORTH KOREA'S CULTURAL AND RELIGIOUS ROOTS

10. Quoted in Savada, *North Korea, a Country Study,* p. 82.

11. Jon Carter Covell, *Korea's Cultural Roots.* Elizabeth, NJ: Hollym International, 1982.

12. Quoted in Savada, *North Korea, a Country Study,* p. 79.

13. Quoted in Savada, *North Korea, a Country Study*, pp. 68–69.

14. Quoted in Savada, *North Korea, a Country Study*, p. 68.

CHAPTER 5: LIFE AND CULTURE IN CONTEMPORARY NORTH KOREA

15. Quoted in Ron Gluckman, "Cinema Stupido," *Asiaweek*, September 1992. www.gluckman.com.

16. Lonely Planet, "North Korea: Culture." www.lonelyplanet.com.

17. Quoted in Greg Constantine, "Singing for Korean Unification," *BBC*, June 27, 2003. http://news.bbc.co.uk.

18. Quoted in Constantine, "Singing for Korean Unification."

19. Quoted in Savada, *North Korea, a Country Study*, p. 88.

CHAPTER 6: NORTH KOREA IN DISTRESS

20. Quoted in Simons, *Korea: The Search for Sovereignty*, p. 243.

21. Quoted in Oberdorfer, *The Two Koreas*, p. 395.

22. George W. Bush, "President's 'State of the Union Address,'" Washington, DC, January 29, 2002. www.whitehouse.gov.

23. Quoted in Associated Press, "North Korea's Official Radio Backs Off Nuke Report," November 15, 2002.

CHRONOLOGY

B.C.

1100–108

The ancient state of Choson rules on the Korea Peninsula.

A.D.

300s

The Three Kingdoms develop on the Korea Peninsula (Paekche, Koguryo, and Silla).

668

After years of conflict among the Three Kingdoms, the kingdom of Silla emerges victorious.

936–1392

The Koryo dynasty rules Korea.

1392–1910

The Choson, or Yi, dynasty rules Korea.

1910

Japan officially annexes Korea, beginning a period of four decades of brutality and repression for Koreans as subjects of a Japanese colony.

1919

Mass protests of Japan's colonization of Korea, known as the March First Movement, occur throughout Korea.

1945

Korea is freed from Japanese occupation after Japan is defeated in World War II. Korea is occupied by Russia in the north and the United States in the south.

1948

The Republic of Korea is created in the south on August 15. On September 9, the Democratic People's Republic of Korea is proclaimed in North Korea and Kim Il Sung, backed by the Soviet Union, is chosen as leader.

1950

On June 25, the Korean War begins when North Korean troops invade South Korea.

1953

The Korean War ends with an armistice agreement on July 27, and a 2.5-mile-wide Demilitarized Zone (DMZ) is created just north of the 38th parallel, separating North and South Korea.

1956

Kim Il Sung announces a three-year plan of economic development and completes it ahead of schedule, achieving a quick economic recovery from the war.

1962

Aid from the Soviet Union declines, and North Korea begins its own military-buildup campaign.

1974

Invasion tunnels dug by North Korea under the DMZ are discovered. North Korea attempts to assassinate South Korean president Park Chung Hee, but fails.

1976

Without provocation, North Korean guards attack a group of UN security workers at a UN checkpoint in the DMZ.

1980

Kim Jong Il, Kim Il Sung's son, is named head of the North Korean government.

1983

In October, North Korean agents attempt to assassinate South Korean president Chun Doo Hwan with a bomb. The president was not harmed, but the bomb kills seventeen members of the South Korean cabinet.

1985

North Korea signs the Nuclear Non-Proliferation Treaty (NPT), promising not to develop or obtain nuclear weapons.

1987

North Korea completes construction of a thirty-megawatt, gas-graphite nuclear reactor. North Korea probably removes enough plutonium from this in the late 1980s to build at least two nuclear bombs. In November, agents of North Korea sabotage a Korean Airlines plane, killing all 115 passengers.

1989
The United States detects evidence that North Korea is developing nuclear weapons.

1991
The Soviet Union collapses, leading to increasingly serious economic problems in North Korea.

1993
On March 12, North Korea withdraws from the NPT and refuses to allow further inspections, causing a serious crisis with the United States.

1994
On July 7, North Korea announces the death of Kim Il Sung, age eighty-two. He is succeeded by his son Kim Jong Il. On October 21, North Korea and the United States sign the Framework Agreement, in which North Korea promises to halt its development of nuclear weapons in return for aid in building civilian nuclear reactors and temporary oil supplies.

1995–1996
Floods afflict North Korea, causing agricultural losses and food shortages and requiring the country to appeal for foreign aid.

1998
The food shortages become critical because of a drought that followed the earlier floods. The government of North Korea imposes food rationing. On August 31, North Korea launches a multistage rocket over Japan.

1999
In September, North Korea announces a unilateral ban on missile testing.

2000
During June 13–15, North Korean leader Kim Jong Il and South Korean president Kim Dae Jong meet for a summit in P'yongyang.

2001

In January, U.S. president George W. Bush takes office, suspends diplomatic relations with North Korea, and orders a review of American policy toward the country.

2002

On January 29, Bush announces in his State of the Union address that North Korea is part of an "axis of evil." On October 4, North Korea announces that it is again developing nuclear weapons. On November 13, the United States and its allies cut off fuel oil promised to North Korea under the Framework Agreement. On December 31, North Korea orders International Atomic Energy Agency inspectors to leave the country.

2003

On January 10, North Korea says it is pulling out of the NPT. On February 5, North Korea announces that it has reactivated its nuclear facilities. On April 23, talks begin between North Korea, the United States, and China, but talks end on April 25 after North Korea announces it already has nuclear weapons. On July 9, North Korea announces that it has reprocessed enough plutonium to create six nuclear devices. On August 27–29, a second round of talks are held between the United States, North Korea, Russia, China, and South Korea, during which North Korea threatens to test a nuclear weapon and declare itself a nuclear power.

For Further Reading

Websites

Asian Info (www.asianinfo.org). This website is dedicated to introducing Asian culture, traditions, and general information to the world.

Korean News Service (www.kcna.co). This is the website for the Korean Central News Agency, a state-run agency of the DPRK. It speaks for the KWP and the DPRK government.

Korea Web Weekly (www.kimsoft.com). This is an independent, nonpartisan, nonprofit website on all things Korean: history, culture, economy, politics, and military—since 1995.

U.S. Central Intelligence Agency (www.cia.gov). This is a U.S. government website for the CIA, providing geographical, political, economic, and other information on North Korea.

The Washington Post (www.washingtonpost.com). This is the website for a major American newspaper published in Washington, D.C., that provides up-to-date news on events in North Korea.

WORKS CONSULTED

BOOKS

Donald N. Clark, *Culture and Customs of Korea.* Westport, CT: Greenwood Press, 2000. An introduction to the Korean people, their culture, and daily life, with information about how history shaped Korean culture (but focusing on modern South Korea).

Jon Carter Covell, *Korea's Cultural Roots.* Elizabeth, NJ: Hollym International, 1982. This book examines Korea's cultural history, focusing on shamanism, Buddhism, and Confucianism.

Bruce Cumings, *Korea's Place in the Sun.* New York: W.W. Norton, 1997. This is a history of North Korea from its ancient beginnings into the 1990s, written by a well-known authority on the country who often has been critical of U.S. policy toward North Korea.

Chuck Downs, *Over the Line, North Korea's Negotiating Strategy.* Washington, DC: AIE Press, 1999. A detailed analysis of North Korea's negotiating style from the end of the Korean War to the late 1990s.

Takashi Hatada, *A History of Korea.* Santa Barbara, CA: American Bibliographical Center—Clio Press, 1969. A classic history of Korea written by a Japanese scholar and historian, this book covers Korea's history up to the Korean War and the creation of two separate nations.

Russell Warren Howe, *The Koreans: Passion and Grace.* New York: Harcourt Brace Jovanovich, 1988. This book looks at Korean culture, focusing primarily on South Korea.

Wanne J. Joe, *A Cultural History of Modern Korea.* Elizabeth, NJ: Hollym International, 2000. This is an in-depth study of Korean culture from ancient to modern times, with a focus on modern South Korea.

Ilpyong J. Kim, *Communist Politics in North Korea.* New York: Praeger, 1975. Though published in 1975, this book nevertheless provides a useful analysis of the Communist system as it was implemented in North Korea, including discussion of issues such as government structure, mass mobilization campaigns, and economic-development strategies.

Korean Overseas Information Service, *Focus on Korea: Korean History.* Seoul, Republic of Korea: Seoul International, 1986. Traces the history of Korea from ancient times to the founding of North and South Korea.

———, *Korea: Its History and Culture.* Seoul, Republic of Korea: Jungmunsa Munhwa, 1996. This book examines the history of Korean culture.

Andrei Lankov, *From Stalin to Kim Il Sung.* London: Hurst, 2002. This well-researched book focuses on the history of North Korea from the end of World War II to 1956, when opponents of Kim Il Sung staged the only known challenge to his regime.

Donald Stone Macdonald, *The Koreans.* Boulder, CO: Westview Press, 1996. This is a new edition of the author's original 1988 introduction to Korea, discussing the culture and politics of both North and South Korea.

Koon Woo Nam, *The North Korean Communist Leadership, 1945–1965.* Tuscaloosa: University of Alabama Press, 1974. Traces the Communist influence on North Korea, from the time of the Japanese occupation of Korea to the early decades of the regime of Kim Il Sung.

Don Oberdorfer, *The Two Koreas.* Canada: Basic Books, 2001. This is a readable history of modern North Korea from the time of its creation until the year 2000, which marked the first summit between the two Korean leaders.

Han S. Park, *North Korea, the Politics of Unconventional Wisdom.* Boulder, CO: Lynne Rienner, 2002. A study of the *Juche* political philosophy as it developed in North Korea under the leadership of Kim Il Sung by a leading expert on the topic.

Andrea Matles Savada, ed., *North Korea, a Country Study.* Washington, DC: Government Printing Office, 1994. This is a Library of Congress study and report on North Korea, providing a good overview of its history, society, economy, government, military, and foreign policy.

Geoff Simons, *Korea: The Search for Sovereignty.* New York: St. Martin's Press, 1995. This is a valuable history of North Korea covering early Korean history as well as the development of modern North Korea following the Korean War.

Chong-Sik Yoo and Se-He Yoo, eds., *North Korea in Transition.* Berkeley: Institute of East Asian Studies, University of California at Berkeley, 1991. Although this book was published in 1991, it contains several essays on topics relevant today, such as the changes brought on by the collapse of the Soviet Union and North Korea's search for a national identity.

PERIODICALS

Associated Press, "North Korea's Official Radio Backs Off Nuke Report," November 15, 2002.

Current Events, "Homecoming: Family Reunions Spark Hopes for a United Korea," October 11, 2002.

Erik Eckholm, "North Korea Presses Demand for Direct Talks with U.S.," *New York Times,* January 31, 2003.

Daniel Goodkind and Loraine West, "The North Korean Famine and Its Demographic Impact," *Population and Development Review,* June 2001.

Michael R. Gordon and Felicity Barringer, "North Korea Wants Arms and More Aid from U.S.," *New York Times,* February 12, 2003.

Nicolette Jackson and Sean Healy, "Desperate Escape: The Backbreaking Work of North Korean Women," *New Internationalist,* September 2002.

Paul Kerr, "U.S. Sends Conflicting Signals on North Korea," *Arms Control Today,* September 2002.

Marc Lerner, "North Korea Weapons a 'Nuclear Nightmare,'" *Washington Times,* January 17, 2003.

John J. Lumpkin, "US Assesses North Korea's Military," Associated Press, January 9, 2003.

Johanna McGeary, "Look Who's Got the Bomb," *Time,* October 28, 2002.

Oil Daily, "N. Korea Blames Breach on US," November 22, 2002.

David E. Sanger, "North Korea Says It Holds Nuclear Card," *San Diego Union-Tribune,* July 15, 2003.

Orville Schell, "In the Land of the Dear Leader," *Harper's Magazine,* July 1996.

Notra Trulock, "North Korea's Nuclear Threat," *Insight on the News,* May 20, 2002.

United Press International, "N. Korea Blasts U.S. Nuclear Strategy," March 13, 2002.

INTERNET SOURCES

Associated Press, "Diamond Mountain, North Korea," 2000. www.tkdunlimited.org.

John R. Bolton, "U.S. Under Secretary of State for Arms Control and International Security," speech in Seoul, South Korea, August 29, 2002. http://usinfo.state.gov.

Bureau of Democracy, Human Rights, and Labor, U.S. Department of State, "Democratic People's Republic of Korea, Country Reports on Human Rights Practices—2001," March 4, 2002. www.state.gov.

George W. Bush, "President's 'State of the Union Address,'" Washington, DC, January 29, 2002. www.whitehouse.gov.

Mike Chinoy, "North Korea's Propaganda Machine," March 1, 2003. http://edition.cnn.com.

CNN, "Starved N. Koreans Eating Grass to Survive," June 21, 2002. www.cnn.com.

Greg Constantine, "Singing for Korean Unification," *BBC,* June 27, 2003. http://news.bbc.co.uk.

Ron Gluckman, "Cinema Stupido," *Asiaweek,* September 1992. www.gluckman.com.

Joseph Hong, "Korean Studies," University of California at Berkeley, http://socrates.berkeley.edu.

Human Rights Watch, "Briefing to the 59th Session of the UN Commission on Human Rights: Democratic People's Republic of Korea." www.hrw.org.

Gaurav Kampani, et al., "Overview of North Korea's Ballistic Missile Program," Center for Nonproliferation Studies, Monterey Institute of International Studies, 2002. http://cns.miis.edu.

Korea Web Weekly, "July 10 Hwang Jang Yop Press Conference," 1997. www.kimsoft.com.

———, "Kim Il Sung University: The First University of the People," October 1, 1996. www.kimsoft.com.

Lee Wha Rang, "N. Korea Nuclear Arsenal," *Korea Web Weekly.* www.kimsoft.com.

Lonely Planet, "North Korea: Culture." www.lonelyplanet.com.

Eric S. Margolis, "North Korean Bombshell," *American Conservative.* www.amconmag.com.

Mu Shim Sunim, "A Return to North Korea," *The Kwan Um School of Zen.* www.kwanumzen.com.

"North Korea: North Korean Sports and Recreation." www.1up travel.com.

People's Korea, "Fifth Winter Asian Games in Aomori, DPRK Takes Part in Winter Asian Games, Wins Two Medals," 2003. www.korea-np.co.

———, "Korean Athletes March Together in Pusan Asian Games," 2002. www.korea-np.co.

VNC Travel, "P'yongyang." www.vnc.nl.

White Mountain, "Mount Paektu in North Korea," September 2, 2003. www.whitemountain.com.

Willi's Korea, "Mount Paektu, der hochste Berg Koreas." www.willi-stengel.de.

Wisconsin Project, "North Korea Missile Update 2000." www.wisconsinproject.org.

INDEX

PICTURE CREDITS

About the Author

Debra A. Miller is a writer and lawyer with an interest in current events and history. She began her law career in Washington, D.C., where she worked on legislative, policy, and legal matters in government, public interest, and private law firm positions. She now lives with her husband in Encinitas, California. She has written and edited numerous publications for legal publishers, as well as books and anthologies on historical and political topics.